Hello Angela.

Hope you are well, please
enjoy a copy of my latest book.
can you Please post about it on
much appreciated.

16.01.25

CHEZ MOI

SIMPLE RECIPES
FROM MY HOME KITCHEN

DANIEL GALMICHE

PRELUDE

You could be the greatest chef ever to have lived, and could have racked up Michelin stars like confetti, yet still the greatest love of cooking food is, and has always been, for friends and family. For me, the greatest meals in your life are the ones cooked at home and based around your home cooking, all whilst enjoying each other's company.

Take my dish of a lifetime, that's one of my late Granny Smith's bacon sandwiches, simply cooked, using the best bacon, super soft bread, and of course, lashings of butter. My Mum's Sunday roasts would be in the top three too, as would be my Auntie's shortbread that used to just melt in your mouth.

What I am trying to get to is that, even the best chefs love this home style of food, and there in Daniel 's, is one that I have admired and tasted his food for a long time.

Being French of course, means that food is in your DNA, but that's just the start of what has become a great career for Daniel, classically trained as a youngster to work in, and alongside, some of the very best in the business.

As a chef myself too, I see like me, Daniel has come full-circle, and he is now settled into the very food he and I both love. If you are thinking this book is going to be classical French, then think again. As like many of us at our age, we have the benefit of experience and travel. Travel is vital in a cook's search. For not only great food, but great knowledge too. What Daniel has done with a passion, is put all of this down on paper, food from his travels, dishes from his childhood and mostly great food from his life and family.

I've known Daniel for 30 odd years, and we have shared many a great meal and story over the kitchen table, also side by side at my house when filming the Saturday show. He is more than welcome anytime, as I love his food. The quality of Daniel's cooking is second to none and is now available for you to follow and enjoy like I do.

"Chez Moi" is where Daniel's real heart for great food and home cooking is, and it's the perfect book for you to enjoy with your friends and family, from a genius in the kitchen.

Enjoy.

James Martin

Photo courtesy of ITV James Martin Saturday Morning/Blue Marlin Television.

CONTENTS

CHEZ MOI (MY HOME)

It is such a lovely feeling when going back home. The moment you open the door, you are back in a familiar environment, a safe place where you feel great, and there is a sense of freedom. A place where you can express yourself with no effort needed and be able to think differently than when in a professional kitchen (now talking for me, as my trade). Here in CHEZ MOI, I can cook those dishes we all love and have shared for generations. Dishes are passed on from grandmother to mother, to daughter, and so on.

I can almost recreate them blindfolded without even thinking. I know for sure it will delight everyone and bring back memories. Everyone is hoping to have those favourites, and I'm looking forward to reminiscing and bringing back those stories told by our elders. Our children wait for them, and their children will do the same. I love that complicity, that exchange that leads to fun around the table, laughter, and much more.

So, hopefully, in this book, you will find all those recipes, and who knows, perhaps some are already your favourites. If not, you just have to cook them, and you might adopt some for your family's enjoyment.

Happy cooking, chez vous!!!

Daniel Galmiche

Daniel
Galmiche

DEDICATION

I must say that 2021 and 2022 have been very hard for reasons that many of you know. But I also have been fortunate to have so many friends and family who have supported me and wished me well. You do not realise how much you helped me. You know who you are on that journey, and I thank you very much.

But I particularly want to thank someone special. Someone who, when we first met, understood my situation and what I went through. She has helped me with her support, friendship, fun personality, wit and love. I also think she knows how much she has lifted my spirit and brought a spring to my step-smiling again, happy again. She became my best friend.

Her help with this book has been very important, especially when, like me, she loves food, so imagine when the time came to taste the dishes-particularly the pastry recipes if I recall. Gourmand, she is, too.

ELISE, this dedication is for you, with lots of love and passion.

Thank you for being special in my life, my partner, and for being you.

LE PRINTEMPS (SPRING)

The one season we are waiting for after all the cold months, and the first of the four seasons. During that time, days slowly get longer until the 21st of June, the longest day of the year, when a celebration of summer arrives.

Spring is also a time of growth and renewal, which we can witness all around us. Nature is blooming and blossoming, the smell of honey travelling from early flowers is released, and the last late frost eventually disappears; this is when nature wakes up. Now we can enjoy the First, asparagus coming out, and then it's time for the Jersey Royal potatoes, forced rhubarb, and, later, strawberries. Everything is on the move; it is time now to let the sun in and start to enjoy!!!

Goat cheese, chicory radish and orange salad

Serves: 4
Preperation time: 25 minutes

INGREDIENTS

1 small bunch chives, cut into 5 cm\2 in. batons

1 tbsp picked chervil leaves

150 g/5½ oz Golden Cross goat's cheese (or St Maure if you can get it), crumbled

1 small orange, zest and juice reserved

1 small bunch of radish, washed, not peeled, sliced

1 tbsp small croutons (if you want)

2 large chicory, washed and pat dry

DRESSING:

1 tbsp honey

1 tbsp balsamic vinegar

3 tbsp extra virgin olive oil

Sea salt and freshly ground black pepper

This is definitely a salad to try, as it's very interesting and different! We used to have a version of this at my aunt's house-she would send us into the garden to pick up radish during the season and add some chicory as well. We used to bring loads back and prepare them with my uncle. Marcel was his name. He would then make the lardons himself, using the salty fat to make the dressing. He often used his old knife, with a blade that was so thin from sharpening it with a big stone on a wheel, but it was ideal for cutting lardons. My mum used to make it at home, but it was never as good. I guess he had made the salad so long that he had perfected it.

Here, I've added a lovely goat's cheese to go with the chicory and radish, which matches it very well, and took the lardons away. The addition of the orange brings a slight tangy accent to it, along with the sweet balsamic vinegar. Simply delicious!

DIRECTIONS

1. Arrange the salad directly in one large bowl. Arrange the chicory like a rosace, then sprinkle the radish slices gently onto the plates. Scatter the crumbled goat's cheese over the top, then add the chive batons and chervil fronds. Next, scatter the orange zest over it, and then finish with some croutons.

2. Whisk the honey, reserved orange juice, vinegar, and olive oil together in a small bowl until it is almost opaque, or you can blitz it with a stick blender, then season it with salt and black pepper. Drizzle all over the salad and serve immediately. It's a lovely summer dish to serve with a glass of Viognier.

Classic nicoise salad with herbs, olives, anchovies and tuna.

Serves: 4
Preperation time: 30 minutes
Cooking time: 20 minutes

INGREDIENTS

1 tin of beautiful small artichoke in oil, stem on, drained, cut in four lengths

1 tin of great quality tuna in oil, drained

1 small tin of anchovies in oil, drained

4 boiled eggs, peeled, cut in 4

4 small tomatoes, cut into wedges

1 red onion, cut into fine slices

2 small cos lettuce, cut into large pieces

80 g/2 oz black pitted olives

A few basil leaves

A few sprigs of chives cut in baton

DRESSING:

1 large shallot, finely chopped

1 garlic clove - use for rubbing the wooden bowl, as it is normally done

3 tbsp of great olive oil

Sea salt

Freshly ground black pepper

Classic nicoise salad is the perfect Spring/Summer recipe, as I love the South of France, but here I want to make the classic, which does not have green beans or potatoes added much later, as an alternative. So, we will use small black olives for this: artichoke, tuna, anchovies, boiled eggs, tomato, and crispy lettuce. All this is in an earth dish, in the middle of the table, on the terrace, in the warmth of late spring or early summer, with family around, a fresh glass of rose de Provence in hand.

A good chat and laughter-what more do we need?

DIRECTIONS

1. So, to make the dressing, first rub a wooden bowl with the garlic clove.

2. Mix the shallots with the olive oil, season with salt and pepper, and keep that dressing aside.

3. In a bowl, put together the cos lettuce and the artichoke, which, if you want, you can cut quickly and pan fry to a lovely golden colour. Add tomato and red onions, anchovies, the tuna broken into pieces, and the egg quartered and olives.

4. Drizzle the dressing on the top, and finally, tear the basil leaves into pieces on the top of the salad, the chives, serve, and enjoy.

5. If desired, you can add a few drops of lemon juice, but that was not in the original recipe. No vinegar, please!!

NOTE: This salad is normally made in a wooden bowl and the garlic is used to rub inside the bowl. But here, you can see I did not have one, so if you do have one, it makes a big difference.

Chargrilled chicken salad with boiled eggs

Serves: 4
Preperation time: 25 minutes
Cooking time: 30 minutes

INGREDIENTS

4 free-range small chicken breasts

2 medium size cos lettuce

1 x 12 quail eggs

2 tbsp of sherry vinegar

2 tbsp of mayonnaise

1 tsp Dijon mustard

2 sprigs of chervils

2 sprigs of tarragon, leaves only

2 slices of sourdough bread, cut into cubes and roasted

1 shallot chopped thinly

1 tsp of chopped mild chilli

Sea salt and freshly ground black pepper

50 g/2 oz butter

3 tbsp olive oil

1 lemon juice and zest

I find potato salad can be a bit heavy on its own, so adding a lovely grilled chicken breast brings a touch of barbecue flavour, which is welcome when grilled. Add fresh herbs, such as chervil, which I really love but are difficult to find. It's a shame as it is so good in a salad! Now add eggs and a sherry vinaigrette, and you will have a great salad to share with friends and family. I prefer a vinaigrette mix with some mayonnaise, as it will keep the salad nutty and fresher. Finish with tarragon leaves and croutons.

DIRECTIONS

1. First, preheat oven to 180 C/360 F/gas 5.

2. Put a medium-sized nonstick grilled pan over medium heat and add olive oil. When slightly smoky, add the pre-season chicken breast to the grilled pan to mark it, and skin first. When that is done, about 3 minutes, just crisscross it the other way to have a lovely pattern on the skin. When ready, put in the preheated oven for about 25 minutes or until cooked enough.

3. When ready, keep it aside in a warm place wrapped in grease-proof paper.

4. Meanwhile, hard boil the quail eggs, or if, like me, you prefer them soft-boiled and a bit runny, fill a small saucepan with water and bring them to a boil. Add a teaspoon of vinegar to the water, as this will make it easy to peel when ready. Place the quail egg in a ladle, slowly slide carefully in the water, cook for 4-5 minutes, keep it slightly soft in the middle, refresh when ready, peel, and keep aside.

5. To prepare the vinaigrette, put the shallot chilli in a bowl, add the mustard, vinegar, and oil, season with salt, add the mayonnaise, whisk to combine, and keep dressing aside.

6. Now, put this lovely salad together. Cut the washed lettuce and place in a large bowl. Cut the warm grilled chicken breast lengthwise into a thick strip, place it nicely in different ways on the top of the salad, and cut the quail egg in half. They should remain almost soft-boiled. Throw in the tarragon leaves, drizzle with the lovely, tasty dressing, and finally, throw in the sourdough croutons and squeeze a few drops of lemon and zest. Enjoy this gorgeous, still-warm grilled chicken salad.

Glazed chicory, thyme and goat cheese tart

Serves: 4
Preperation time: 25 minutes
Chilling time: 30 minutes
Cooking time: 20 minutes

INGREDIENTS

6 large chicory (endive)

75 g/2½ oz butter

60-90 ml/2-3 fl oz/¼-1/3 cup + 1 tbsp water

250 g/9 oz ready-made puff pastry

2 tbsp honey

¼ tsp picked thyme leaves

1 lime, zest and the juice

1 tbsp of chopped flat parsley

Half a goat cheese log, crumbled

1 green apple cut into baton, keep in lemony water so they do not go black

sea salt and freshly ground black pepper

This is another starter I really enjoy. I am glad to say that nowadays, we are seeing more and more people using salad as a cooked starter or serving it as a substitute garnish with a meat or fish dish. Finally! It is making its way to the table, hooray!!

Here, I use chicory, which is very versatile as a vegetable-it can be made as a gratin, braised, roasted, or in a tart. You can pre-roast the chicory (endive) and finish it with some fresh thyme. Those three ingredients will lift the chicory to a new height. Make sure that you do not forget to sprinkle the apple on the top at the end. You will be surprised by this lovely dish and how well it works.

Then, when still warm, add the goat's cheese, which is slightly crumbled on the top.

DIRECTIONS

1. Grease a 20 cm/8 in. tart tin with butter. Roll out the pastry on a lightly floured surface until it is about 3 mm/1/8 in. thick and 2 5cm/10 in. in diameter. Line the tin with the pastry, taking care not to stretch it. Press down gently to push out any bubbles and roll the rolling pin along the edge of the tin to trim off the excess pastry. Prick the base with a fork and chill for 25-30 minutes to prevent the pastry from shrinking during cooking.

2. Meanwhile, make the filling. Cut the chicory in half lengthways, remove the bitter stem part, and discard it. Heat a large sauté pan on medium heat. When warm.

3. Add 50 g/1¾ oz of the butter and the chicory, cut side down. Cook for 4-5 minutes until they are slightly coloured but not burnt-the butter must remain light golden brown.

4. Add the water-no more than 1 cm/½ in. high in the bottom of the pan-then scatter over the lime zest and remaining butter. Finish with the lime juice, freshly ground black pepper and a touch of sea salt.

5. Tip: You need to cover the pan with a cartouche-this is a piece of parchment paper, cut to just larger than the pan, with a small hole in the centre. This allows the liquid to evaporate but keeps the moisture in and retains the colour of the chicory. As you cover the pan, turn the heat down to a very low simmer and cook for a further 10 minutes until the chicory is very tender and caramelized. Check occasionally to make sure that it's not burning. If it starts to catch, turn the heat down even lower and add a drop of more water.

6. Preheat the oven to 170 C/325 F/Gas 3. When the oven is hot, line the pastry case with baking parchment and fill with baking beans. Bake in the preheated oven for 12 minutes, remove from the oven, and discard the beans and parchment. Return to the oven for 3-5 minutes until the base is just golden. Remove and gently press down on the pastry if it has risen. Turn the oven up to 200 C/400 F/Gas 6.

7. When the tart is blind baked and the chicory is fully cooked, discard the cartouche, carefully lift out the cooked chicory, and set aside on a cloth to absorb any residual liquid. They need to be perfectly dry

8. Add the honey and thyme to the pan and warm through, gently stirring the residual until it all comes together like syrup. Remove from the heat.

9. Allow the chicory to cool to room temperature before placing it into the blind baked tart case-pack them tightly into the case, add goat cheese, and brush the lime honey syrup over the top. Place into the oven and warm through for 3-5 or until the goat cheese is slightly melted.

10. Remove from the oven, then remove from the tin. Scatter apple and herbs over the top and serve warm.

Croque monsieur with roast ham and gruyere cheese

Serves: 4
Preperation time: 20 minutes, plus making salad and vinaigrette
Cooking time: 5-6 minutes, plus grill

INGREDIENTS

4 large eggs

400 ml/14 fl oz/scant 1,5 cup full-fat milk

1 long farm bread, not baguette or farmhouse loaf bread, cut diagonally into 8 thick slices

150 g/5 oz butter

8 slices of farm roast ham

100 g/3 oz of gruyere cheese or other mature hard cheese, grated

Sea salt and freshly black pepper

200 g/6 oz of prepared bechamel

This one is a croque Daniel, haha! This is how we did it at home, generally on Sunday evening. We all loved it, the bread remaining from Saturday or that morning from the baker, but it was always better from the day before. Of course, you can use sourdough too, but what better than to add some rich bechamel sauce and finish under the grill when it all starts running with a slight golden colour... Wow!! What a treat!!, ANOTHER ONE PLEASE!!

DIRECTIONS

1. Put the eggs and milk in a bowl, season with salt and pepper and whisk well, then transfer to a shallow dish. Soak each slice of bread in egg mixture, turning three or four times so that it takes in the liquid.

2. Melt half the butter in a large frying pan over a medium heat. When foaming, add bread and cook for 2 minutes until golden brown and a little crispy, then turn the bread over and add the rest of the butter. Cook on the other side for 2 minutes. If you are using a small frying pan, cook in batches using a quarter of the butter for each batch.

3. Put 1 slice of ham and some of the grated cheese on each slice of bread, and when the cheese starts to melt, add the other slice of bread on top of the cheese. Flick the croque monsieur over once more and cook for up to 1 minute until hot through. Now put one or two spoons of bechamel and flash it under your oven grill until it starts to be golden in colour.

4. Serve hot cut in two with a lovely salad of lamb lettuce, perfect!!

Pan-fried plaice goujons in a chilli, lime and spring onion garlic mayo

Serves: 4
Preperation time: 25 minutes
Cooking time: 8 minutes

INGREDIENTS

2 medium-sized plaice, filleted, skin off, cut into goujons

1 thyme sprig

2 red chillies, 1 split lengthways, deseeded and finely chopped

300 g/10 oz/3 cups panko breadcrumbs

1 tsp dried chilli flakes

200 g/7 oz/2 cups plain flour

3 eggs beaten

4 tbsp sunflower oil

80 g/4 oz unsalted butter

4 tbsp very finely chopped flat leave parsley

GARLIC MAYONNAISE:

2 egg yolks

1 tbsp white wine vinegar

1 tbsp Dijon mustard

150 ml/5 fl oz/scant 2/3 cup sunflower oil

2 garlic cloves, crushed to a paste

1 lime, zested

Sea salt and freshly ground black pepper

During the plaice season, this is one of my favourite dishes to share and cook. We are very lucky in the UK as the plaice is very good and plentiful. It is a very versatile fish, tasty, simple, and of good value. It is served as tapas or a sharing platter but also in many other ways. I love to do goujons in breadcrumb at home with a hint of lime zest and chilli. Panko breadcrumbs are widely available in all stores. Follow this delicious recipe, and I tell you, you will do it again, and next time, make sure you do a double batch for your friends!

DIRECTIONS

1. First, prepare the plaice; if not, ask your fishmonger to do it.

2. Then, reserve on a kitchen towel in a cold place.

3. To make the garlic mayonnaise, put the egg yolks, vinegar, and mustard into a medium bowl and whisk it together. Drizzle the oil in, a little at a time, whisking continuously. Add the crushed garlic and lime zest and season with salt and black pepper.

4. Put the breadcrumbs into a food processor with the dried chilli and blitz to a semi-fine powder. Pour onto a plate. Break the eggs into a bowl and whisk with the remaining chopped fresh chilli. Pass the plaice goujons through the flour, then drop into the chilli egg, and finally into the chilli breadcrumbs, tossing to coat on all sides.

5. Heat a medium frying pan over medium-high heat, add half the butter, and when it's foaming, add half the plaice goujons and pan fry on each side until golden brown and crunchy, for about 2-3 minutes. Drain onto kitchen paper, then repeat with the remaining butter and goujons

6. Pile the plaice onto a big plate, scatter the parsley over the top, and put it in the centre of the table with the garlic mayonnaise. Let everyone help themselves.

7. Just remind yourself that you probably will need more next time, as it is very delicious. Also, you can grate a bit of lime zest on the top for fresherness.

8. It's so good, but be quick, too, as the others will not wait for you!!

Pan-roasted sea trout, braised chicory, lime, soya and herbs

Serves: 4
Preperation time: 30 minutes
Cooking time: 15 minutes

INGREDIENTS

4 medium-sized chicory, cut in half lengthways
1 lime, zest and juice
4 x 160 g/ 5 oz pave of sea trout
1 pinch roasted crushed black pepper
2 tbsp olive oil
2 tbsp of soy sauce
60 g/2 oz butter
1 sprig of flat parsley, washed and chopped
1 small bunch of spring onions
1 tbsp of chopped chilli
1 tbsp balsamic vinegar
6 tbsp of water

Since working with the Norwegian Seafood Council, I have learnt how to appreciate this delightful fish for its taste and the versatile ways you can cook it. Sea trout goes very well with many different ingredients. It is like salmon, but it is more delicate. This dish can be cooked in smaller quantities (eg 2 paves instead of 4). In this recipe, I will use chicory, herbs and soy. Late Spring is perfect for this fish, so it needs nice accompaniments. Whatever you use, beware of the strength of the spices; they can destroy this lovely dish and your dinner, too!

Chicory will be my choice here, roasted in the casserole with the fish, adding a bit of soya, spring onions and lime. This will make a very tasty dish, and a fast dinner too!!

DIRECTIONS

1. Season the sea trout all over with salt and black pepper.

2. Place an oven-proof frying pan, large enough to take the garnish in, or a cast-iron casserole over medium heat. Add the olive oil and half of the butter. When foaming, add the fish skin side down and roast for 2/3 minutes or until golden brown.

3. Throw in the chicory to roast into a light golden colour, but keep turning it on all sides gently until the colour is even. Now it is time to turn the fish over, so adding the liquid does not soften the skin and keeps it crispy. It should be by now about 5/6 minutes altogether, as you do not want any to be overcooked. Then add the water, soya, and vinegar and continue to braise for a few minutes until the liquid has reduced by a third. Throw in the last of the butter and swirl to combine-this will finish the sauce nicely, making it lovely and shiny.

4. Finally, throw in spring onions, chilli, lime juice, zest, and herbs. You should have just enough liquid to serve on the fish by that time. Love this one-pan dish. It is a very quick dinner, 10-12 minutes, served with jasmine rice or spinach on the side, which is a delight and very tasty!

5. Note: You can also add mushrooms; they go well, too.

Sea trout with broad beans and fresh mint beurre Blanc

Serves: 4
Preperation time: 30 minutes
Cooking time: 25 minutes

INGREDIENTS

4 x 140 g/5 oz pavé sea trout, skin on
1.4 kg/ 3 lb broad beans in pods
1 punnet of micro mint or fresh mint leaves
2 tbsp of olive oil

MINT BEURRE BLANC:

250 g fresh unsalted butter (room temperature)
75 g/2 oz banana shallots, finely chopped
1 small bunch of fresh mint
100 ml/3 fl oz/scant ½ a cup good white wine
Salt and freshly ground white pepper

What a lovely Spring recipe! When the broad beans season is here, you will appreciate the freshness of the broad beans, kept slightly crunchy and only partially crushed, but the real star is the sea trout, kept pink in the middle, and the final touch will be the mint in the beurre blanc. What a delightful dish, so tasty!

DIRECTIONS

1. Take the fresh broad beans and shell them. Blanch them very quickly, then refresh them in ice and set them aside before shelling the second skin, which makes a big difference.

2. To make a classic beurre blanc, melt 30 g/1 oz of butter in a small pan over medium heat, and fry the shallots for 2 minutes until just softened. Add the stock and a few mint leaves. Bring to a simmer and cook for 2-3 minutes. Now let it infuse for a few minutes in a warm place, as you want freshness and not strength.

3. After that time, start to gradually add in and whisk the remaining softened butter, a few cubes at a time, and keep whisking until the butter is incorporated, before adding more. The sauce will split if the temperature changes too quickly, so as you are whisking, you should see a foam of tiny bubbles form on the top of the mixture and when all butter is added. The sauce should be pale in colour and light in consistency. Similar to a very thin custard, it should just coat the back of a spoon. This will take you 10-12 minutes.

4. At this point, season to taste, add a few drops of lemon juice, cover, and keep in a warm place.

5. Place a sheet of grease-proof paper in a large non-stick pan and drizzle over a touch of olive oil. When warm but not smoking hot, place the sea trout in the pan, skin down first. Cook to give the fish a lovely colour, almost crispy but not burnt, then place the pan in a preheated oven at 160oC for 2-3 minutes. Ensure the sea trout isn't overcooked; it needs to stay nice and pink in the middle.it should take overall 8 to 12 minutes for the fish.

6. To serve, warm up the broad beans, crush half of them with a fork, and place them in the middle of the plate. Position the sea trout on top of the crushed beans and scatter a few whole broad beans around the fish. Finish, drizzle with mint, beurre blanc, and add top with a few micro mint or chopped mint leaves.

NOTE: This technique of cooking on grease-proof paper is something people should adopt, especially when you have an old sauté pan, so not only does the fish not stick to the pan, but also you do not need as much fat, and the fish skin will be very crispy. Make sure you keep it pink in the middle so you can appreciate its flavour even more. It's so great.

Fresh crab meat risotto, with spring onions

Serves: 4
Preperation time: 20 minutes, plus 45 minutes
for stock
Cooking time: 35 minutes

INGREDIENTS

1.2/42 fl oz litres of fish stock

100 g/3.5 oz of fresh crab meat, picked

60 g/2 oz brown crab meat

30 ml/1 fl oz olive oil

1 large shallot or small onion, very finely chopped

60 ml/2 fl oz white wine

300g / 10 oz of risotto rice, carnaroli if possible

1 tbsp mascarpone

1 tbsp crème fraiche

2 tbsp chopped spring onion

Grated Pecorino cheese to serve or mature cheddar

During the British crab season, there is no better than a lovely light risotto. The taste of brown and fresh crab meat in a risotto is superb. It brings a lovely fresh seawater taste with a touch of saltiness, is creamy and nutty, and is perfect with a beautiful grated cheddar or pecorino. Make sure you have enough, as the gourmand will have two helpings!! It is one of my partner Elise's favourite recipes among plenty. In fact, she is a gourmand, haha!

DIRECTIONS

1. In a medium pan over medium heat, pour in the fish stock, bring to a boil, then reduce the heat to low and keep it at a simmer.

2. Heat the olive oil in a large, heavy-based pan over low to medium heat, add the shallot or onion, and sauté for two to three minutes or until soft and slightly golden. Add the rice to stir, add the wine and let it evaporate to remove the acidity. The best thing is to use a good wine you will drink with your risotto, and never use a bad wine for cooking! Then, add the brown crab meat and stir. Add one ladle of the stock and stir continuously until almost all is absorbed. Repeat this, gradually adding stock until the rice is cooked: approximately 18-20 minutes. The grain should be plump first and not too dry, as I like the risotto to be loose and light, although this is personal.

3. Now it is time to add the mascarpone and the crème by folding in gently so you do not damage the rice. You should see it becoming shiny and loose. Then, fold in the white crab meat, spring onions and serve while hot. If necessary, just before you serve, add another 1 or 2 spoons of the hot stock to keep it slightly loose, so it is much better to enjoy it that way. Have pecorino grated and ready, and sprinkle over your risotto. Delicious! I love this one and do it often.

NOTE: Make sure you get some good quality crab meat from your fishmonger rather than from a tin, as they are a world apart when it comes to flavour.

Stuffed tomato with mince lamb scented with rosemary flower

Serves: 4
Preperation time: 25 minutes
Cooking time: 35-40 minutes

INGREDIENTS

4 beef tomatoes

400 g/14 oz minced lamb

2 sprigs of rosemary, chopped ,or the flowers or lavender flowers too

sea salt and freshly ground black pepper

2-3 tbsp olive oil

In this book, you will come across two "farci" recipes. It is very French but also very Mediterranean-a great one to eat on the terrace on a warm evening with a rose wine. Classic rosemary-scented lamb, and you are in Provence.or if you prefer, some lavender flowers. I did it with a roasted leg of lamb, just sprinkled on top. Here, though, it is mixed with minced lamb and the flesh of the fresh tomatoes and baked in the oven. It's a great family dish-perhaps a fresh garlic baguette for the juices.

DIRECTIONS

1. Preheat the oven to 170 C/325 F/Gas 3.

2. Cut the top off the tomato, only about ¾ of the way down, and reserve.

3. Turn the tomato upside down and press to squeeze the seeds out, discarding the seeds.

4. Scoop the flesh out of the inside of the tomato, roughly chop and mix with the minced lamb.

5. Add some of the rosemary, then season well with salt and freshly ground black pepper.

6. Also, season the inside of the whole tomato and place it onto a small oven tray lined with grease-proof paper.

7. Divide the mixture into 4, then roughly roll each piece into a ball and press into the whole tomatoes so that the meat comes slightly above the top of the tomato, about 1 cm.

8. At that point, keep the tomato lid on the side.

9. Drizzle the tomato with some olive oil, then place in the oven to bake for 30 minutes. After that time, place the remaining lid on top of each tomato and bake for about 10 minutes.

10. Check with the help of a fine skewer into the centre to see if the meat is cooked through-if it comes out clean, the meat is cooked. You also should have a fair bit of juice. Scoop some out of the tray into a small pan, then reduce by half, and add the rest of the olive oil. Make sure you keep the tomato warm. Serve then enjoy with a fresh garlic baguette for the juices.

Pineapple beignets (fritters) with chilli, mango salsa, lime and tarragon

Serves: 4
Preperation time: 25 minutes
Cooking time: 25 minutes

INGREDIENTS

50 g/2 fl oz caster sugar

2 large semi-ripe mango, peeled and cut into small dice

3 pinches of freshly cut chilli, half of it for the beignet mix

1 sprig of tarragon, no stalk, leaves only

1 small lime, half of the juice and full zest

BEIGNET:

1 large pineapple, skinned, cut into 4 lengthways, core removed and cut into small chunks about 1.5 cm/2-3 in. thick

125 g/4½ oz plain flour

2 eggs, yolks and whites separated

1 pinch of salt

125 ml/4 ½ oz bitter beer

25 ml/1 fl oz sunflower oil

25 g/1 oz caster sugar, plus extra for dusting

For me, pineapple is the perfect fruit for a beignet, as it is called in France (fritter).

It has the right amount of sugar and acidity, which makes it special. Serve with a lovely mango salsa with a hint of chilli and a fresh tarragon leaf, which will be even better.

DIRECTIONS

1. For the salsa, mix the diced mango with half of the chilli, the lime juice, and half of the zest; it will help to soften the fruit. Place onto a serving dish, and keep it in a cool place covered with a film.

2. Heat a sunflower oil-filled deep-fat fryer to 170 C/325 F or fill 2/3 full a 12.5 cm/5 in. deep, wide sauté or saucepan with clean sunflower oil and heat to 170 C/325 F.

   NB - you really do need to use a thermometer for this. At 170 C/325 F, the oil doesn't burn or smoke at all. I prefer to use sunflower oil as it has a cleaner taste in the end. Also it can take higher temperatures in case it gets too hot by mistake. Just be aware though.

3. Place all the pineapple chunks onto a clean tea cloth lined tray and spread out into a single layer. Fold the tea cloth over to cover the pineapple and press down firmly to remove the maximum amount of liquid. Leave to dry like this while you prepare the mixture.

4. Mix the flour, egg yolk, salt, butter and sunflower oil together to make a thick, lovely smooth paste. When that is done, whisk the egg whites and caster sugar together to soft peaks in a separate bowl. When the meringue is ready, gently fold it into the beer paste.

5. Place a piece of pineapple onto a long skewer, metal or wood, and dip quickly into the beignet mix until completely coated. With a fork, at a low height over the hot oil, push the pineapple off the skewer into the oil. Repeat with the rest of the pineapple-you most likely want to cook six pieces at a time only. When the beignet starts to float to the top of the surface, you will need to carefully turn them over and continue to cook until they are golden brown on each side and lovely and crisp-this should take about 4-5 minutes, turning them occasionally. They will be slightly crunchy when they are ready. Remove from the oil with a slotted spoon and place directly onto a kitchen paper-lined plate. Dust immediately with some caster sugar.

6. Serve the beignet in the centre of the table, sprinkle with the remaining lime zest, and add some chopped tarragon to the salsa. Mix well, enjoy with the fritter, and eat straight away! Be aware it is so good that you will definitely want more.

Caramelised pineapple, dark rum, vanilla and pink peppercorn

Serves: 4-6
Preperation time: 30 minutes
Cooking time: 30 minutes

INGREDIENTS

2 of the smallest pineapples you can find, peeled in four segments, core removed

300 ml/11 fl oz dark rum

1 small vanilla pod, cut in half widthways then lengthways, seeds scraped

110 g/4 oz light soft brown sugar

50 g/2 oz butter

½ tsp pink peppercorns, gently crushed

1 lime, juice and zest

What can we say? It seems everyone I speak to loves pineapple desserts. I do, too. For this recipe, it's ideally best done with baby pineapples, but if not, as small a pineapple as you can find would be great as they are generally sweeter. The addition of rum and pink peppercorn is gorgeous. It will bring the whole dessert to new heights, and finally, the grated lime zest and juice make for a lovely finish.

DIRECTIONS

1. Roll the pineapples in the light, soft brown sugar to coat all sides.

2. Scrape the vanilla seeds into the rum and mix well.

3. Heat the butter in a large nonstick frying pan over medium heat, add the pineapples, and roast them gently on each side. Add the vanilla pods and continue roasting until the pineapples start to caramelise. When they get golden brown, add 4 tbsp of the vanilla rum. Do not flambé, but let it reduce while roasting, basting the pineapple all the time until it just forms a light syrup and starts to caramelise. Repeat these two more times, 4 tbsp at a time, then add the pink peppercorns and cook until you have a lovely light caramel brown thick syrup that coats the pineapple. This whole process should take 25 to 30 minutes.

4. When it is all caramelised, but not burnt, add half of the lime juice and throw in the zest. The fragrance will rise straight away.

5. Now, it is time to serve each large segment on a warm dessert plate and drizzle the syrup over the top. I recommend a lovely cake or a simple lime and coconut ice cream.

Dandelion flower cake, lime ,orange and thyme infused syrup

Serves: 6-8
Preperation time: 30 minutes
Cooking time: 45-55 minutes

INGREDIENTS

Juice and zest of 1 lime

Half the juice of an orange and zest

1 handful fresh dandelion flowers, picked, sepal and bracts removed

1 tsp baking powder

170 g plain flour, plus extra for dusting

4 medium eggs

150 g/5 oz/1 cup caster sugar

A pinch of salt

7 tbsp double cream

60 g/2.5 oz unsalted butter, melted, plus extra for greasing

THYME SYRUP:

2 tbsp caster sugar

Juice of 1 orange

Juice of 1 lime

2 sprigs of thyme

These three wonderful ingredients transform that classic cake recipe into something special. The scent of lime zest, orange and thyme brings sweet, bitter and delicate freshness to your tongue. The dandelion flowers are often forgotten but were well used in the past, and they are still used nowadays as an infusion. It all goes so well together! We love it, so I say, prepare the tea, I am coming!!

DIRECTIONS

1. Preheat the oven to 170 C/325 F/Gas 3. Butter and flour a 1 kg loaf tin or use a silicone cake mould dust with flour.

2. Infuse the thyme in the cream in a small pan over low heat. Heat gently until the cream is just starting to simmer, then remove from heat and set aside. Cover with cling film for 15 minutes to infuse.

3. Meanwhile, Sift the flour and baking powder into a bowl. Put the eggs, sugar, and salt in another large bowl and use an electric whisk for 8-10 minutes until light, thick, and pale. At that point, it should almost be double the volume.

4. Strain the thyme-infused cream, then fold in the egg and sugar mixture, along with the lime, orange juice and zest.

5. Then, add the sifted flour and baking powder and fold gently together. Finally, fold in the melted butter and half of the dandelion flowers. Now, pour the mix into the prepared cake tin or silicone cake mould.

6. Bake for 35-40 minutes or until a skewer into the centre comes out clean. If not quite ready, bake for a further 5 minutes and check again.

7. In the meantime, make a syrup with the lime, lemon, wild thyme and sugar in a saucepan over low heat. Then, after the sugar has dissolved, turn the heat up to medium and cook until there is just enough left to drizzle on the cool cake-about 4 spoonsful.

8. Sprinkle with the rest of the dandelion flowers. Slice and serve.

9. A good Earl Grey tea should do the trick.

L'ETE (SUMMER)

Ah! Finally, it is the hottest of the four seasons, but it is also the time to go outside and enjoy a great lunch on a terrace along the river or an early dinner with friends or family.

Nature is offering a bounty of products we have waited for. We also start to see some premature yellow leaves on some of the trees, telling us that Autumn isn't far away, but before that happens, let's enjoy what's on offer: Artichoke, broad beans, green beans, peaches, nectarines, sea trout, crab, plaice, etc., and a lot more. Cooking at that time of year is so much fun and light. The terrace is ready, the BBQ is on, the family is waiting, and rosé wine is on ice. So what are you waiting for?! Go on.

Eggs cocotte with sauteed mushrooms, and thyme croutons

Serves: 4
Preperation time: 20 minutes, plus 1 hour infusing
Cooking time: 20-25 minutes

INGREDIENTS

CRISP:

110 ml/4 fl oz olive oil

2 sprigs of thyme, leaves picked

1 frozen loaf of baguette or farmhouse bread

HEN OEUF EN COCOTTE:

40 g/1½ oz butter, softened to brush the ramekin

4 large hen eggs or pheasant eggs, as during the season, they are so delicious, but you will need two each in that case

275 ml-300 ml/10-11 fl oz whipping cream-must be straight from the fridge

Sea salt and freshly ground black pepper

4 sprigs of thyme, leaves picked from one sprig

200 g/7 oz chestnut mushrooms, roughly chopped-then they will need to be washed once or twice and patted dry

1 tsp olive oil

½ small shallot, finely diced

½ garlic clove, finely diced

Oeuf cocotte is traditionally done with hen eggs and in a bain marie. It used to be a touch heavy as it was often made with double cream and often overcooked, so it is necessary to watch the timing closely so that the egg yolk remains soft and runny within the mix. By using whipping cream, you will lose the heaviness. You can serve it with the crouton scented with thyme for a lovely earthy flavour and pan-fried chestnut mushrooms.

DIRECTIONS

1. First of all, make the crisp. Place the olive oil and thyme leaves into a saucepan and warm through-only heat until about 45 C. Remove from the heat and leave to infuse for a good hour, then pass through a fine sieve and decant back into a bottle. You can keep this in your store cupboard and use it for tomato tarts, dressings, etc.

2. Preheat the oven to 140 C/275 F/Gas 1.

3. Allow the bread to defrost for 5-10 minutes until just softened enough to cut it.

4. Take 4 slices, 3 mm thick and lay them onto a grease-proof or silicone-lined tray. Brush with the thyme olive oil until just coated, then place another sheet of grease-proof or silicone on top and finish with another tray that will fit inside the base tray to keep the crisp flat. It will also allow it to cook more evenly. Place in the oven and bake for 8-10 minutes until golden brown. Check it halfway through, as you really don't want it to colour too much too quickly. Remove and set aside to cool between the trays until needed.

5. Turn the oven up to 180 C/350 F/Gas 4.

6. Place a piece of grease-proof paper or kitchen towel into the base of a small roasting tray. Brush 4 x 150 ml/5 fl oz ramekins with the softened butter, making sure that all the inside is coated in butter. Crack 1 egg very carefully into each ramekin, then pour the cream over the top to just cover, season with salt and black pepper, then add a sprig of thyme.

7. Place in the oven for 8-9 minutes. Do remenber to put water half way up the side of ramekin dish. To make sure the yolk remains soft, you can cover the ramekin dish, and after the 8 minutes, uncover and let it bake for a further 2 minutes.

8. Time will be a bit less if using pheasant egg.

9. Meanwhile, bring a saucepan of water to the boil, add the chopped mushrooms, then return to the boil and quickly drain onto kitchen paper and pat dry.

10. Heat a frying pan until medium-hot. Add the oil, shallots and garlic and sweat over a gentle heat until softened but not coloured. Turn the heat up, add the mushrooms and sauté quickly until just wilted-no more than 2 minutes.

11. Season with salt and black pepper to taste, then add the remaining picked thyme.

12. As the cocotte comes out of the oven, spoon the mushrooms on top, then place them onto a plate. Serve the crouton alongside to dip into the egg! You can also make soldier croutons if you prefer, of course.

13. Gorgeous!!

Tiger prawns and sea bream ceviche with apple, chilli and tarragon

Serves: 4
Preperation time: 20 minutes, plus 1 hours marinating

INGREDIENTS

20 medium to large fresh-shelled tiger prawns, cleaned and waste track removed

2 limes, zested and juiced

1 medium red onion, peeled, chopped, diced

1 red chilli, seeded and finely chopped

1 garlic clove, crushed

1 tsp chopped tarragon

1 tbsp chardonnay vinegar

Sea salt

1 Granny Smith apple, halved, cored, and sliced into matchsticks

So, what is ceviche? It is originally a Spanish word and is a great speciality of Peru, Ecuador, and Chile. It is basically raw marinated fish or shellfish, always prepared with plenty of citrus, herbs, onions, shallots, etc. But the shellfish must be fresh or freshly frozen, and again, it's best to trust your fishmonger; he will really have the expertise you want. Enjoy it served with mango, perhaps, or an avocado and red onion with flat parsley. I also add a touch of garlic here, but you do not have to. I just love it!

DIRECTIONS

1. Reserve 4 whole tiger prawns, then cut the rest into 1 cm/½ in. thick chunks and place into a bowl. Add the whole tiger prawns, the lime zest, juice, and vinegar, then fold gently together. Cover it, then marinate it in the fridge for about 1 hour.

2. Remove from the fridge, take out the whole prawns, then add the tarragon, chilli, onion, garlic, all but 1 tablespoon of the apple, and fold together. Divide the mixture between four glasses and place the whole langoustine on the edge of the glass. Scatter the last of the apples over the top and serve straight away.

3. Great served with a chilli, tarragon or even garlic mayonnaise.

Pan fried salmon with lemon butter sauce, braised cabbage with chilli

Serves: 4
Preperation time: 20 minutes
Cooking time: 50 minutes

INGREDIENTS

1 Savoy cabbage, cut in 4, hard stems removed, chopped

4 x 120 g/4 ¼ oz salmon fillet

60 ml/2 fl oz/1/4 cup whipping cream

100 g/3 ½ oz butter

1 lime, zested and juiced

Sea salt and freshly ground black pepper

1 small chilli, chopped into small dices

This is a good family dish, easy and quick, but the cooking time needs to be precise. Again, a probe would be good to use, but if you don't have one, follow my exact timing, as it will give you perfectly cooked salmon. You don't want to overcook salmon; it needs to be cooked to medium unless you have specific dietary requirements. Then, that's a different matter.

Chefs are always talking about quality, and it's very important to have as fresh products as you can possibly get. That's why if you have a fishmonger close by, it's the place to go. Likewise, a local butcher knows what it is all about; they have the expertise, which makes all the difference to the end dish.

DIRECTIONS

1. Start by preparing the savoy cabbage, chopped and washed.

2. Bring a large saucepan of salted water to a boil, blanch the cabbage for about 3 minutes, then lift out straight into a bowl of iced water for 1 minute. Remove and place directly onto a kitchen cloth to dry.

3. Now it's time to make the lime butter. Pour the cream into a small saucepan, place it over high heat, and bring it to a boil. As it comes to a boil, remove it from the heat, add 1 tablespoon of cold water, then whisk in the butter, a little at a time-if it gets too thick too quickly, add a little lime juice to thin it down, then continue until it is all incorporated. It should be lovely, yellow and shiny but not heavy. Check the seasoning, add the lemon zest, cover with cling film, and set aside in a warm place while making the salmon.

4. Season the salmon with salt and pepper on both sides.

5. Heat the oil in a frying pan over medium heat and place the salmon skin down for 4-5 minutes until crispy and golden brown. Then flip it over gently and finish for 2/3 minutes. Make sure you keep it rose in the middle, as much tastier and healthier.

6. While this is ongoing, just put the cabbage back in the pan and warm it with a bit of olive oil, half of the chilli, and a pinch of salt. Cover and keep warm until the salmon is ready.

7. Now, ready to serve the cabbage, place the salmon on top, and drizzle the sauce with the rest of the chilli. Enjoy!!

NOTE: In here I have made the butter sauce with cream at the beginning, to help you so it does not split, but in a original recipe, there is no cream.

Curry spiced hake parcels with lime, coriander and coconut sauce

Serves: 4
Preperation time: 15 minutes
Cooking time: 12 minutes

INGREDIENTS

1 small red chilli, halved, seeded and julienned

4 x 150 g/5½ oz hake loin, skin off, pin boned

Sea salt and freshly ground black pepper

20 g/¾ oz butter

1 tbsp olive oil

60 ml/2 fl oz/¼ cup coconut milk

60 ml/2 fl oz/¼ cup fish stock

100 ml/3 ½ fl oz/1/3 cup + 2 tbsp whipping cream, lightly whipped

2 tbsp coriander, half for the parcel, the rest for the sauce

1 tsp lime, zest and juice

I love cod. It's a fish that I cook a lot at home, but with that fish becoming slowly endangered in the UK, it is good to look for other great alternatives and different ways to cook it. Here my choice of fish is hake loin.

I often like to cook "en papillote in a parchement (parcel)"; it is fun, fresh, fast, and delicious. I have tried so many different combinations. In my last book, the recipe that I did became very popular. I know some of my friends have done it again and again many times, which is a good sign. In this one, lime brings some freshness without overpowering the hake, as the balance of the dish will be lost, and you do not want that to happen. Then, all that's left to do is make a light creamy sauce with coconut milk and coriander.

DIRECTIONS

1. Season the hake on both sides with salt, black pepper and lime zest. Heat a medium nonstick frying pan over medium-high heat, add the butter and olive oil, and when foaming, add the hake, on the plummy side of the fish side down and pan fry for 3-4 minutes until slightly golden and crispy.

2. Put four 46 x 25cm/18 in. x 10 in. rectangles of greaseproof paper on your work surface. Next, you need to put some coriander on one half of the paper so that you can fold the other half over it afterwards, dividing it equally between the four sheets, then place the hake golden and crispy side on top. Fold the paper over the filling, then fold along the edges to seal securely. Make sure the parcels are well sealed so that no liquid is lost. Put the parcels on a baking tray and bake for 8 minutes. Remove from the oven and leave to rest for 2 minutes before opening.

3. While the fish cooks, make the sauce. Heat a small sauté pan over medium heat, pour the fish stock and coconut milk in and bring to a boil, then reduce the heat and simmer gently until reduced by half, for about 4-5 minutes. By now, the fish should be ready. Carefully open one side of each parcel, pour the cooking juices into the sauce, and then place the parcels straight onto the serving plates. Whisk in the whipped cream, return to the boil, remove from the heat and check the seasoning. Add the rest of the coriander and a bit of lime juice.

4. You've now got two options! You can either serve the parcels en papillote at the table with the sauce in a sauce boat or jug, or you can open the parcels, slide the filling out onto a serving plate and spoon the sauce over the top. Your choice!

NOTE: If your fish portion is bigger than that of my list, add more time to cook.

Serves: 6
Preperation time: 50 minutes
Cooking time: 45 minutes

INGREDIENTS

100 g/3 oz carrots, washed, peeled, cut into small cubes

1.2 litres/40 fl oz/4 cups fish stock

1 large onion, finely chopped

1 tbsp curry powder

200 g/7 oz potatoes, washed, peeled, cut into small cubes

200 g/7 oz turnips, washed, peeled, cut into small cubes

4 tomatoes, cut and deseeded

1 tbsp tomato puree

3 tbsp plain flour

200 ml/7 fl oz single cream

100 ml/3 fl oz white wine

Sea salt and freshly ground white pepper

2 tbsp chopped fresh parsley

1 tbsp chopped chervil

2 tbsp olive oil

25 g/1 oz butter

200 g/7 oz plaice fillet, slice in strip fillet

200 g/7 oz sea trout fillet cut into large strips

This is really a full meal on its own, as there is lots in it.

Perfect for late chilly summer nights, I prefer sea trout rather than salmon as the flavour is more delicate, nutty, and tastier.

It is also delicious with monkfish or sea bream. By the way, do not be put off by the ingredients list, as it is easy to make!

DIRECTIONS

1. Sift the flour into the cream and mix well to ensure there are no lumps.

2. Heat the olive oil and butter in a heavy-based large saucepan over medium heat. When foaming, throw in the onions, carrots, and turnips and cook until softened and golden.

3. Then, add potatoes, curry powder, and tomato puree and mix gently. Pour in the white wine and evaporate by a third, then add fish stock and bring to a boil. Add the fresh tomato; when they are almost cooked, carefully add the flour and cream mix you prepared and gently incorporate it into the soup by swirling it.

4. Finally, throw in the fish strips and simmer for a few minutes or until cooked but still together.

5. At that point, when cooked, the fish will be delicate. Keep it slightly firm, check the seasoning together, and add the herbs.

6. Serve hot. You can add garlic sourdough croutons and a nice beer to drink it with or the rest of the white wine.

Pot roasted guinea fowl legs with beer and baby turnips

Serves: 4
Preperation time: 15 minutes
Cooking time: 50-60 minutes

INGREDIENTS

1 tbsp olive oil

1 sprig of thyme

4 guinea fowl legs

250 ml/10 fl oz good quality beer

500 ml/18 fl oz chicken stock

12 small turnip/navet, peeled and cut into quarters

I have always enjoyed the delicate, nutty flavour of guinea fowl. I am using the leg here, as this poultry is often forgotten, but it is so good. Keep the breast for a casserole later, giving you another meal. Like in this recipe, the beer will bring an original taste to your guinea fowl. You will discover a beautiful dish by trying this one. Add a touch of curry powder or even smoked paprika for a twist.

DIRECTIONS

1. Heat a medium-sized casserole dish over high heat, add a splash of oil, and the guinea fowl legs skin side down. Roast until a lovely golden brown colour all over the legs. Pour off any excess fat, then deglaze with the beer, cooking until the liquid is reduced by about half, then add the chicken stock and the thyme.

2. Cover with a lid then move the lid over so there is a gap of 2.5 cm/1 in. on one side to allow the steam to evaporate. Simmer gently for 15 minutes, then add the baby turnips or navet, replace the lid and cook for another 15 minutes until the guinea fowl is cooked through and the turnips/navet are tender.

3. Remove the legs and turnips/navet from the pan and place them onto separate plates, but keep it warm.

4. Return the casserole to the heat and reduce the liquid to a glaze. When it is reduced enough, return everything to the pan and heat back through, carefully coating the guinea fowl. Check for seasoning.

5. Great served with pilau rice.

NOTE: *You can use purple navet in a season cut in segments. They are delicious and underuse, perfect for that dish, even better with a pork dish, and better finished in the sauce.*

Stuffed courgettes, jasmine rice, melted comte cheese

Serves: 4
Preperation time: 35 minutes
Cooking time: 50 minutes

INGREDIENTS

4 large courgettes

150 g/5½ oz jasmine rice

1 large onion, diced

4 tbsp olive oil

100 g/3½ oz butter, chopped

1 small bouquet of garni

300 ml/10½ fl oz/scant 1¼ cup vegetable stock

1 quantity of Tomato coulis from a good supplier, or make yours if you prefer

60 g/2¼ oz Comte cheese, grated

In my youth, I remember Mum loved making stuffed vegetables, and so did we when it came to eating that great dinner. She generally used leftovers.

But we really liked it; the mix was fantastic-stuffed potatoes, tomatoes, etc., all on the same tray with different fillings. Served with a freshly made tomato coulis with herbs tossed through at the last minute, I remember it like it was yesterday. It was delicious.

Here, jasmine rice brings a nice fragrance, along with Comte cheese, my favourite. Of course, this is my region, so it brings back memories.

DIRECTIONS

1. Preheat the oven to 150 C/300 F/Gas 2.

2. Place a saucepan of water onto simmer, with a steamer insert on top, big enough to hold all the courgettes.

3. Trim either end of the courgette, then very carefully, cut lengthways down the courgette, trimming off only the smallest amount so that the courgette will sit flat on the work surface without wobbling. Then, cut lengthways again, taking off the top third and setting it alongside. Use a teaspoon to scoop out the inside of the courgette, taking care not to make a hole in the bottom or break the sides, and set it to one side. If the courgette doesn't have too many seeds, chop the flesh and put it in the pilau.

4. Season the inside of the courgette with salt and black peppercorn, and place the lid back on the courgette. Place it on a sheet of cling film and roll up tight, keeping the lid on top of the courgette. Place in the steamer for 12-15 minutes on a simmer. Turn the heat off, remove the lid of the steamer, and leave it to rest while you make the rice.

5. Heat a medium frying pan over medium heat. Add the olive oil, onion, chopped courgette if using, and the bouquet garni and sweat for 5 minutes until just softened, then turn the heat down and add the rice. Fold in gently, then sweat for 3-4 minutes. Add the vegetable stock and bring to a simmer. Season with salt and black pepper, dot the butter over the top of the rice, then cover with a cartouche or lid and place in the oven for 15 minutes. Check whether the rice is tender and the liquid is absorbed. If the rice is not quite tender, return to the oven for another 5 minutes and check again.

6. Turn the oven to grill.

7. Run a fork gently through the rice, remove the bouquet garni, and check the seasoning. Remove the courgette from the cling film and turn onto a kitchen towel to drain. Turn it back up and place it on a baking dish. Fill them with the rice, pressing down lightly, then place a large spoonful of tomato coulis over the top of the rice, sprinkle the Comte over the top, then place the whole dish under the grill for 2-3 minutes, until the cheese is melted and starts to colour. Remove from the oven, top with the lid and serve with the extra tomato coulis.

Marmalade of tomato confit, basil cream, langue de chat biscuits

Serves: 4
Preperation time: 30 minutes, plus cooling
Cooking time: 35 minutes

INGREDIENTS

CHERRY TOMATO MARMALADE:

250 g/9 oz vine cherry tomatoes, cut in half

75 g/3 oz caster sugar

100 ml/3½ fl oz/1/3 cup + 1 tbsp water

6 basil leaves

1 tsp good balsamic vinegar

450 g/1 lb natural goat's milk yoghurt

1 lime, zested

LANGUE DE CHAT BISCUIT:

100 g/3½ oz soft goat butter

100 g/3½ oz caster sugar

3 egg whites, kept separate

125 g/4½ oz strong flour

½ vanilla pod, seeded

6 tbsp goat crème fraiche

Here, we are talking about Langue de chat, a dry biscuit we normally serve in the afternoon with coffee or tea. In fact, you can often buy them in a metal tin of mixed biscuits, as they are still very popular nowadays, but of course, many people make them too.

I am a lover of goat's produce, and I've wanted to do this recipe for a while now. I have made an all-goat langue de chat, and to go with it, marmalade with a difference, vine cherry tomato marmalade. It is gorgeous. It is sweet and has a touch of acidity with the goat's yoghurt, basil, balsamic and lime zest. I think you will really have fun making this dessert. It's completely different and original.

And the good thing is that it is now possible to find all goat dairy ingredients in the supermarket or independent shops.

DIRECTIONS

1. Start by making the marmalade. Place the tomatoes, sugar, water, 1 basil leaf, and the balsamic in a sauté pan and set it over medium heat. Bring to a boil, then reduce the heat and simmer for 20-30 minutes until thickened and syrupy, just like a marmalade. Remove from the heat and spoon into a bowl, cover and leave to cool.

2. When fully cold, strain through a fine sieve into another bowl to collect the juices, which you then mix with the goat's milk yoghurt. Set the tomato confit aside, then roughly chop the last basil leaf and mix with the yoghurt until just combined.

3. Preheat the oven to 200 C/400 F/Gas 6.

4. Now, make the langue de chat-beat the butter and sugar together in a kitchen mixer or with an electric whisk in a bowl for a good 5 minutes until the mixture is lightened and the sugar dissolves. You will have to add the egg whites, one at a time, as the mix will split if you add them all at once, and they need to be well incorporated before you add the next one. After that, sift the flour into the mix and slowly fold in, then beat in the vanilla seeds and crème fraiche and mix well until the mixture is soft, pale and creamy. Spoon into a piping bag.

5. Butter and flour on a nice flat baking tray, then tap and discard any excess flour. Trim the end of the piping bag off to about 1 cm/½ in. diameter, then carefully pipe 7.5 cm/3 in. lengths onto the tray. There needs to be a gap of about 10 cm/4 in. between each biscuit as they will really spread during cooking. Place in the oven and bake for 5-6 minutes, but you will need to turn the tray, front to back, very quickly after 3 minutes. After 6 minutes, you will see that the centre is still very pale, then it changes colour to a dark golden brown as it gets to the outside-this is exactly what you want! Don't think that the middle isn't cooked yet.

6. Remove it from the oven, and the biscuit will become crunchy as it cools down.

7. If you want, when just out, roll them straight away in a cylinder shape. It's fun!!

8. To serve, take four small sundae glasses and spoon the confit tomatoes into the bottom, top with the yoghurt, then finish with a little grated lime zest and fresh remaining basil leaf in each of the glasses. Serve the Langue de chat on the side.

Cocoa infused sourdough bread with roasted nectarine and thyme

Serves: 4
Preperation time: 15 minutes
Cooking time: 25 minutes

INGREDIENTS

75g/3oz butter

4 nectarines, halved, stoned and cut into
8 segments (not too ripe)

3 tbsp of great local honey

20 g/¾ oz cocoa powder

200 ml/7 fl oz of full-fat organic milk

2 eggs

50 g/2 oz caster sugar

4 thick slices of large sourdough bread, about
2.5 cm/1 in. thick, or brioche if you prefer

25 g/1 oz toasted almonds

3 tbsp crème fraiche

1 tsp fresh thyme leaves

A regular dessert at home, as Mum always kept the old sourdough bread, which is the origin, but also can be done with a lovely brioche, use a great cocoa powder, as it does make the difference, and one which is bitter, not sweet, as the overall dessert will also be too sweet. Alternatives can be peaches or pears, but you will see how nice they are!!

DIRECTIONS

1. Preheat the oven to 180 C/350 F/Gas 4.

2. In an ovenproof sauté pan, on medium heat, melt half the butter and sauté the nectarine until golden brown on both sides. When golden, add 2 tbsp of the honey, toss to coat, then transfer to the oven and roast for 2-4 minutes or until it is soft but not over.

3. Remove and set aside on a plate, but leave the oven on.

4. Mix half the cocoa powder with the milk, the eggs, and sugar in a wide, shallow bowl, then add the bread two slices at a time and soak it on both sides. Place the bread onto a tea cloth to drain slightly.

5. Heat a large frying pan over medium heat, add the remaining butter and honey, and when the two are just melted together, add the bread and pan fry on each side until it is just golden brown and slightly crispy. Be careful not to let the bread burn, as honey and cocoa powder can burn easily if heated too high, but you still want to achieve a lovely golden colour and crispness. You must do this in a large frying pan; it's just not possible in a toaster!

6. Place the "pain perdu" onto a shallow baking tray, then top it with the roasted peaches, a sprinkling of toasted almonds, and a dusting of the remaining cocoa powder. Place in the oven to heat through for 2-3 minutes. While that's heating, mix the crème fraiche with the thyme leaves.

7. Serve the pain perdu with the thyme crème fraiche on the side, or if you don't fancy that, a nice vanilla ice cream for a treat!

Roasted yellow plums, pistachio biscotti, limoncello cream

Serves: 4
Preperation time: 30 minutes
Cooking time: 40 minutes

INGREDIENTS

PISTACHIO BISCOTTI:

100 g/3½ oz butter

75 g/2½ oz caster sugar

2 eggs, plus 1 egg and 1 tbsp water for brushing

½ lime, zested

20 g/¾ oz ground pistachio

1 pinch of salt

½ tsp baking powder

½ vanilla pod

20 g/¾ oz toasted whole pistachio

PLUMS (YELLOW, LARGE):

10 plums, halved, stoned, then cut into 6 segments each

100 g/3½ oz caster sugar

1 tbsp limoncello

LIMONCELLO CREAM:

30 g/1 oz icing sugar

1 egg

125 g/4½ oz mascarpone, brought to room temperature

125 ml/4 fl oz/1 cup whipping cream

2 tbsp limoncello

The texture of yellow plums is lovely and delicate, which is why I have used them here; they come towards the middle of the season. With it, I also thought about a nice biscuit, but what kind could I make for a change? Ah! Why not one with pistachio? It's unusual, perhaps not done as much at home, but it has a good nutty crunch. Then, add some soft pic whipped cream with limoncello liquor whisked in to make it silky; add a touch of black peppercorn, and the dish is complete. Now, the only thing left to do is to serve and see the reaction.i think you will make it again, too nice!!

DIRECTIONS

1. Preheat the oven to 180 C/350 F/Gas 4.

2. Start by making the biscuit-place the butter and sugar into a food mixer or bowl and cream with a paddle beater or electric whisk until it is very pale and fluffy. Add the eggs, one by one, beating in between, then add the remaining ingredients. Continue to mix on a slow speed until the mixture just comes together to form a dough. Scoop the dough onto a lightly floured work surface and form a log about 20 cm/8 in. long and 7.5 cm/3 in. wide.

3. Using the palms of your hands, roll the log until it is about 2.5 cm/1 in. thick, then place it onto a large silicone or grease-proof lined tray-it should just fit. Break the last egg into a small bowl and whisk with a pinch of salt and water. Brush over the top of the loaf, then place it in the oven for 8 minutes. Then turn the tray around front to back, turn the oven down to 150 C/300 F/Gas 2 and cook for a further 20-25 minutes.

4. Meanwhile, make the plums - place a frying pan over a gentle heat, add the sugar and cook slowly until it turns to a light golden caramel. Once more, it is essential that the plums are at room temperature; otherwise, the caramel will block-it will form lumps of hardened caramel, and then it's a matter of starting again! So, add the plums a quarter at a time, mixing into the caramel between each addition. Only when they are all coated do you want to add some more. Cook until they are soft, then drizzle over the limoncello and stir gently to combine. Leave them to cool to room temperature.

5. While the plums cool and the biscuit finishes cooking, whisk the icing sugar and egg together in a large bowl until very light and pale. Mix the mascarpone and cream in a separate bowl, whisk in the limoncello, then fold that into the whisked icing sugar and whisk until the mixture is very smooth and silky but still very soft, only just holding the shape of the whisk.

6. Take the biscotti out of the oven and immediately transfer to a chopping board. Cut either end off the loaf and set aside, then cut the rest into 1 cm/½ in. thick slices and return them to the baking tray. Place them back in the oven and bake for another 5-8 minutes until they are just dry but still only a lightly golden colour.

7. While they bake, crumble the reserved ends of the biscotti into a small bowl- you want pieces about 5 mm/¼ in. big.

8. To serve, you ideally want four sundae glasses. First, place some plums at the bottom of each glass, then top with the crumble. Divide half of the limoncello cream between each glass, then spoon some more plums over the top and finish with the rest of the limoncello cream. Balance one biscotti on the top of each glass, placing the rest on a plate to share in the centre of the table.

Marinated red summer fruits with rosemary cream on sourdough

Serves: 4
Preperation time: 20 minutes
Marinating time: 30 minutes

INGREDIENTS

450 g/1 lb fresh strawberries, washed, hulled, chopped in large slices

450 g/1 lb fresh raspberries a whole.

100 g/3½ oz caster sugar

1 small lime, juice and zest

250 ml/9 fl oz/1 cup crème fraiche

1 tbsp freshly chopped rosemary leaves

300 g/10½ oz fresh sourdough bread in thick slices or brioche if your prefer

2 tbsp of chopped roasted hazelnut

This recipe is so French and has great childhood memories for me. How many times did I pick strawberries and raspberries in my garden as a child? Hundreds, I am sure, and every time, with the same enthusiasm and joy. I was always waiting for that special moment when Mum would say, "Who wants to go pick some fruits for lunch?" I was often the first to answer but probably the last to come back as I was too busy eating them. Anyway, pick, wash carefully, mix with cream and some freshly chopped rosemary, leave to marinate, and then simply crush with a fork. We'd enjoy a big bowl of them with a slice of toasted brioche made with a lovely fresh farm butter, just done so simply like that, and they were so good!

DIRECTIONS

1. Mix the strawberries, cut into large slices, add the raspberries with the sugar and lemon juice in a bowl and leave to marinate in the fridge for 20 to 30 minutes. Remove and add the crème fraiche, then mix delicately. Make sure you do not crush the raspberries as, at that stage, they are a bit fragile. Add the fresh rosemary and stir once more.

2. Serve on sliced, freshly toasted sourdough,(or brioche) then sprinkle with the lime zest and a few roasted hazelnuts. It is so refreshing and very tasty.

NOTE: Tarragon, rosemary flower, goes well too, just be aware tarragon is strong, so be gentle in quantities

Peach, fig, plums in filo parcel, vanilla ice-cream

Serves: 4
Preperation time: 40 minutes
Cooking time: 20-25 minutes

INGREDIENTS

400 g/14 oz filo pastry sheets

Plain flour for dusting

100 g/3 oz butter, melted

400 g/14 oz of mixed peaches, figs, plums, stones out, peach and plums in small segments, figs in 4 so it all cooks together at the same time

1 vanilla pod, cut in half lengthways

2 tbsp of caster sugar

Zest of half a lemon

2 crushed biscotti

Icing sugar for dusting the top

Vanilla ice cream to serve

I love doing this kind of pastry dessert. It is fairly quick and very crunchy, and depending on the season, it can be adapted so easily, adding not only fruits but also herbs, spices, nuts, etc. Here, we will celebrate the end of summer with peaches, figs and plums. Also, a few crushed biscotti help soak the juices, which means the pastry will stay dry. A bit of vanilla pod and star anis also add some great scent and flavours. It is served with a simple vanilla ice cream, perfect for crunching on a sunny afternoon!

DIRECTIONS

1. Preheat the oven to 180 c/350 f/gas 4-5. Unroll the filo pastry, spread it out on a lightly floured worktop, and cut it into 8 rectangles, about 30 cm x 15 cm/12 x 6 in. Brush each pastry rectangle with a coat of melted butter, stacking it on top of the other to create two stacks of four pastry rectangles.

2. By coating each pastry in butter, you will get a beautiful crumbly parcel, and it will not get soggy when the fruits start to release juices during baking.

3. Leave a 3 cm/1 in. wide border along the edges, and arrange the fruit on the middle quarter of both pastry stacks, keeping the remaining pastry free to fold over. Sprinkle with the crushed biscotti, and place the vanilla, star anis sugar, and lemon zest on top.

4. Working with one pastry and fruit stack at a time, brush the edges of the pastry with some of the melted butter left. Fold the pastry over the fruit, then fold the side over the pastry. Now, gently pinch the edges together, make sure they are well sealed, and repeat with the other. You should have two beautiful parcels, both enough for two.

5. Transfer both parcels onto a baking tray, lay them on a greased baking sheet, and sprinkle them with the icing sugar, giving them such a lovely shine during baking.

6. Put in the oven for about 20-25 minutes until golden brown and shiny.

7. Serve warm with vanilla ice cream.

NOTE: *The biscotti biscuits will not only prevent the fruits from soaking the pastry but also add a lovely nutty flavour.*

L'AUTOMNE (AUTUMN)

That most gorgeous season when nature decides to wear those robes of vibrant colours: orange, purple, red, bronze, and gold.

The forest floor is covered with leaves drying and crunching under our feet when walking or even running in them, like when we were younger. To be honest, I still love doing this. It is the season of wild mushrooms, reminding me of when going with my family foraging for them, keeping the place a secret as much as possible.

But a sudden strong wind helping the tree to get rid of the last few leaves is telling us that winter is around the corner, but before that, we can enjoy that season of plenty, from game to root vegetables, to wild mushrooms, autumn truffle, to the last apple and some blackberries remaining, if the weather has been kind enough. And then Halloween, where pumpkin is king, so enjoy the last warm autumn day before the cold arrives.

Shallots tarte tatin, with goat cheese, thyme caramel

Serves: 4
Preperation time: 25 minutes
Chilling time: 30 minutes
Cooking time: 1 hour

INGREDIENTS

375 g/13 oz ready-made puff pastry

200 g/7 oz caster sugar

80 ml water

½ tsp lemon juice

4 sprigs of thyme

7 medium to large banana shallots, peeled, some cut in length, some cut in disk

1 egg, lightly beaten

Sea salt and freshly ground black pepper

100 g/3½ oz fresh soft goat's cheese

1 tsp black onion seed

1 small baby gem, or red lettuce, or rocket leaves

1 tbsp extra virgin olive oil

In my first book, French Brasserie Cookbook, I made a classic tarte tatin with a twist. In this book, I have chosen shallots, not a fruit normally associated with them - banana shallots, more precisely, which have a better sweetness. It is the same idea, principle, and technique. So, to go with this, I have chosen goat's cheese. For me, it's the perfect partner. Also, I have made a single larger tarte tatin, so you can share it in the middle of the table, which is better fun for lunch speciality. It's a lovely outdoor dish served sat on a terrace or in your garden, and I'd serve it with salad leaves, rocket or herb salad. Any of those would go well. The thyme caramel is a delight.

DIRECTIONS

1. Roll the pastry out on a lightly floured surface, then cut out 1 large disk about 22 cm in diameter. Place the pastry on a baking sheet, cover with cling film and chill for 25-30 minutes. This will prevent the pastry from shrinking during cooking.

2. Preheat the oven to 160 C/325 F/Gas 2 ½.

3. Melt the sugar gently in a medium non-stick frying pan with the water and lemon juice, and cook until golden brown, for about 10-12 minutes. When ready, remove it from heat; do not let it burn. Place 2 sprigs of thyme in the bottom centre, then add the shallots, rounded side down into the caramel, and alter the shape. There should be a lovely rosace.

4. Place in the oven and bake for 20 minutes, then remove and turn the oven up to 190 C/375 F/Gas 5.

5. Remove the pastry from the fridge and brush it with the egg wash. Then, carefully place the pastry on top of the shallots, pushing the edges into the dish. This needs to be done quickly as the pastry will melt if you take too long. Sprinkle a little sea salt over the top, then place it back into the oven and bake for 10-15 minutes until the pastry is golden brown and crisp.

6. Remove the tart from the oven and leave to cool for a few minutes. Put an upside-down plate the size of the dish on top of the tart, hold both the plate and dish, flip to unmold onto the plate, make sure you do not burn yourself, and use a kitchen towel - not for the children to do!! Crumble the goat's cheese over the top of the tart and sprinkle with the black onion seed.

7. Mix the rocket or other leaves with the olive oil in a small bowl, then season with a pinch of salt and black pepper.

8. You can serve on the tart or in a bowl in the middle of the table. And that is absolutely superb.

Leek, pancetta and chestnut mushroom pie

Serves: 4-6
Preperation time: 40 minutes
Cooking time: 50-60 minutes

INGREDIENTS

400 g/14 oz leeks, washed and chopped

300 g/10 oz chestnut mushrooms,
washed, cut into cubes

100 g/3.5 oz pancetta, cut in cubes and blanched

200 ml/7 fl oz crème fraiche

1 large egg

2 egg yolks (one for brushing the pie)

Sea salt and freshly ground white pepper

300 g/10 oz savoury pastry (see p.22)

50 g/1.7 oz butter

2 tbsp olive oil

What is it about pie that we love so much? In fact, we could do a British tour and taste the whole of Britain through different pies. It is part of the heritage of this country I choose to live in; it is part of the way I feel through comfort food, simple and delicious. This pie I am making is also a part of my French culture, as we make so many.

DIRECTIONS

1. Take a classic pie tin, non-stick, if possible, but still brush with melted butter, and keep aside.

2. Put the pancetta in a small frying pan over medium heat and fry, stirring occasionally, until starting to be crisp, then remove and pour over a kitchen towel to take off excess fat.

3. In a medium-sized saucepan, put oil and butter. When foaming, throw the mushrooms in and sauté until soft and golden. Add leeks and mix occasionally until soft but keeping the lovely, pale green colour. Remove and keep aside, then add the pancetta to the mix. The leeks and mushrooms should only be slightly softened, not cooked. Keep it in the fridge until needed.

4. Preheat oven to 190 C. Roll the pastry into a lovely large sheet, then cut two discs from it, one larger than the other as it will cover the bottom and side. Place the first disc at the bottom of the tin and make sure it overhangs by about 5 cm; add the cold mushroom mix, leeks, and pancetta inside. Put the pie into a baking tray and chill. Prepare the mix of beaten egg, egg yolk and cream. Whisk it well and season it to your taste. Do not forget to go easy on the salt, as pancetta can be a bit salty. Take the pie out of the fridge, pour the liquid over the mix, carefully cover the filling with the second disc and trim the excess so that it is slightly larger than the tin. Fold the excess of the bottom pastry over on itself and form a ring around to crimp the pie with your thumb and forefinger. Cut a small hole in the pastry in the middle so the steam can escape. Brush with whisked egg yolk all over the top, twice if possible.

5. Score a small design if you wish, or use a fork to draw lines.

6. Place in the oven, cook for 10-12 minutes at 190 C, then lower the oven to 160 C and bake for a further 40-45 minutes. Then remove and check with the point of a knife. If cooked, your knife should be dry out of the pie; if not, put it back for a few minutes and cool down before serving. Delicious with a crunchy salad.

Risotto of roasted mushrooms, leeks, parsley

Serves: 4
Preperation time: 25 minutes, plus 45 minutes
for the stock
Cooking time: 35 minutes

INGREDIENTS

100 g/3.5 oz chestnut mushrooms, washed
and roughly chopped

1 small bunch of leeks, washed, green part
only, chopped

60 g/2.1 oz butter

1 tbsp olive oil

1 large shallot or small onion, finely chopped

60 ml/2.1 fl oz dry white wine

1 litre/35 fl oz vegetable stock

300 g/10 oz risotto rice such as Arborio or carnaroli

1 tbsp mascarpone

1 tbsp crème fraiche

1.5 tbsp chopped flat parsley

Sea salt and freshly ground white pepper

Pecorino to serve, or comte

Another risotto for you. This one is a bit more autumnal, especially if you can get hold of wild mushrooms. It makes a difference in the taste. Roasting the mushrooms will add so much more flavour to the rice. Adding the blanched green part of the leeks is essential for the freshness and earthiness of that dish, finished with flat parsley, bringing a grassy scent.

DIRECTIONS

1. Bring the stock to a boil in a medium-sized saucepan, reduce the heat, and keep it at a simmer. Bring the water to the boil in another saucepan, add a pinch of sea salt, and throw in the green chopped leeks. When water boils again, remove, get rid of water, or use it to add to stock. Refresh it in cold water and keep it on kitchen paper if it is not too salty.

2. Melt half of the butter in a large, heavy-based saucepan over medium heat. Add the shallots and sauté for 2-3 minutes until lightly golden and softened. Then add the rice and stir. Add the white wine and let it evaporate to remove the acidity. Add a ladleful of the stock and stir continuously until it is absorbed. Repeat until the rice is cooked, about 18 minutes. The grain should be plump but still firm.

3. Now add mascarpone and crème fraiche folding in nicely. Check the seasoning, then add the green leeks and parsley, add the sauté mushrooms, which you can do at the last minute, and fold into the rice, too, making sure you keep the rice warm by just adding a ladle at the last minute so it is loose enough. Serve immediately with a lovely pecorino ready to be grated on the top. A wild rocket salad would be a bonus!

Casserole of Autumn vegetables, roasted pears and chestnut mushrooms

Serves: 4
Preperation time: 40 minutes
Cooking time: 50-60 minutes

INGREDIENTS

80g/2¾oz butter

1 tbsp sunflower oil

150 g/5 oz carrots, peeled and cut into 2 cm/¾ in. chunks

150 g/5 oz swede, peeled and cut into 2 cm/¾ in. chunks

2 firm pears, peeled and cut into 8 wedges

2 large banana shallots, peeled and cut into 2.5cm/1" thick rings

110 g/4 oz small chestnut mushrooms, washed, kept whole

150 g/5 oz celeriac, peeled and cut into 2cm/¾ in. chunks

8 unpeeled garlic cloves

150 g/5 oz butternut squash, peeled and cut into 2cm/¾ in. chunks

4 small ratte potatoes, scrubbed and each cut into 3 pieces

2 sprigs thyme

600 ml/20 fl oz/½ cup chicken or vegetable stock

1 tbsp chopped flat-leaf parsley

At home, I often do casseroles of all sorts. It is very much the way my mother cooks, and I really think the flavour comes through differently, as you can control the cooking of the dish much more easily. Autumn is an ideal time of the year for that type of cooking, and I also think the ingredients available are perfectly suited.

As you've seen in the title, I am using chestnut mushrooms, but if you find some wild mushrooms, girolles or ceps, for example, it would be a plus for the taste. Not only do I love them, but they will bring so much to the casserole. The flavour and texture are superb. The key here, though, is not to overcook the ingredients, but after the roasting stage, the magic will be brought by slow cooking them gently together. By trying this recipe, I am sure you will agree, and by doing so, you will discover another different way of cooking.

DIRECTIONS

1. Heat a cast iron casserole over medium-high heat, and add 20 g/¾ oz of the butter and the sunflower oil. When the butter is foaming but not colouring, throw in the carrots and immediately lower the heat, stirring occasionally for about 6-8 minutes until just starting to soften around the edges, with the lid three-quarters of the way across. You need to always pay attention and keep stirring them so they don't colour on any side, but they shouldn't be cooked yet. Add the swede and cook in the same way for another 6-8 minutes.

2. While the swede and carrot are cooking, heat a nonstick frying pan over medium heat. Add 20 g/¾ oz of the butter, and when it's foaming but not colouring, add the pear (if using that option) and shallot and sauté until just caramelised, about 6-8 minutes. The pear should just be tender but not overcooked.

3. Add the mushrooms to the pan with the pears and shallots, then stir and add the thyme sprigs and sauté for another 3-4 minutes over low to medium heat. Season well with salt and black pepper, then remove from the heat and set aside.

4. Return to the main casserole dish now, add another 20 g/¾ oz of the butter, the celeriac, and garlic and cook in the same way for another 6-8 minutes while mixing the whole lot together. None of the vegetables should be fully cooked yet, but they should all look shiny and slightly softened. Add the butternut squash and potato and repeat for another 6-8 minutes. Increase the heat to high, remove the lid, and slowly add the last of the butter to the chicken stock. Keep the casserole over high heat and cook until the liquid has reduced enough to just coat all the vegetables and become lovely and shiny - you need to do this quickly so the vegetables don't overcook. Remove the casserole from the heat, add the pear mixture and flat-leaf parsley, and swirl around to combine.

5. You can serve this on its own just as it is or with a roast venison haunch. Either way, it's a fantastic dish full of goodness.

Roasted duck breast with peach and chicory lettuce

Serves: 4
Preperation time: 30 minutes
Cooking time: 40 minutes

INGREDIENTS

4 medium size chicory, cut in half lengthways

2 unripe white peaches

4 Gressingham duck breasts

1 pinch of roasted crushed Szechuan pepper

2 tbsp sunflower oil

2 tbsp of soy sauce

60 g/2 oz butter

1 sprig of rosemary

200 ml/7 fl oz/½ cup brown chicken stock

2 tbsp sherry vinegar

1 shallot, chopped

Here, I will use Gressingham Duck, but if you can, use wild mallard duck during the shooting season. Your butcher may have some. Female duck is generally more tender. Duck goes very well with lots of different fruits/spices. Here I am using white peaches. When using spices, I always use whole star anise, or if you prefer, vanilla or cinnamon are great alternatives. Just beware of spices strength, they can destroy this lovely dish and your dinner too!

DIRECTIONS

1. Cut the peaches in half, remove the stone, then cut them into four pieces.

2. Preheat the oven to 180 C/350 F/Gas 4.

3. Season the duck breasts with salt and black pepper, then add some Szechuan pepper to the skin side only. Place an oven-proof frying pan, large enough to take the garnish in, or a cast-iron casserole over medium heat. Add the sunflower oil and half of the butter. When foaming, add the duck, skin side down and roast for 4-5 minutes or until golden brown. Turn the duck over and place it in the oven for another 6-8 minutes. The duck should be ready. Remove from the oven, place onto a shallow small baking tray, cover and rest for a few minutes. Turn the oven up a notch. Discard some of the fat from the duck pan, then return it to medium heat.

4. Add the chicory to roast, along with the peaches, into a light golden colour, making sure they do not go too soft. When both chicory and peaches are ready, remove them from the pan and set aside in a warm place. Return the pan to the heat, throw in the shallots, and sweat them for a few minutes until they are soft. Then, deglaze with the sherry vinegar and the soya. Add the chicken stock and the rosemary and cook until reduced by half. Throw in the last of the butter and swirl to combine - this will finish the sauce nicely, making it lovely and shiny.

5. Pour the juices from the rested duck into the sauce, then put the duck back into the very hot oven for 2 minutes to quickly reheat. If the peaches and chicory have cooled too much at this point, they can also be flashed through.

6. Remove the duck from the oven, cut it in half lengthways and divide it between four plates. Spoon the peaches and chicory around the edge of the duck. Pour the juice into the sauce, bring it quickly to a boil, then drizzle over the duck.

Poached chicken with lemon, olives and flaked almonds

Serves: 4-6
Preperation time: 40 minutes
Cooking time: 1 hour 30 minutes

INGREDIENTS

1.5 kg/3 lb/5 oz hen chicken, trussed

4 carrots, peeled, cut in half length way

4 navet turnips, cut into 4 segments

4 Charlotte potatoes cut in half

1 sprig thyme, plus 1 tbsp picked thyme leaves

150 ml/5 fl oz/scant 2/3 cup whipping cream

1 large handful of good stoned black olives

1 lemon, zested and juiced

1 tbsp extra virgin olive oil

1 handful of roasted almond flakes

You will have seen a classic poule au pot in my previous book. However, I have modernised it a little, adding some Mediterranean flavours to it with olives, lemon and almond flakes. Also, you would normally serve the bouillon first as a soup and then the garnish (vegetables) with the chicken as a main course.

Here, I take some of the liquid and reduce it to a sauce. I then add the olives, parsley, and lemon zest, which makes it very refreshing. I hope you enjoy this version, but perhaps you can make both and see which one you prefer. That would be interesting.

DIRECTIONS

1. Place the chicken into a large casserole, cover it with cold water, and bring it to a boil over high heat. When it starts to simmer, skim the foam that rises to the top using a ladle - this helps to keep the soup nice and clear.

2. Add the carrots and cook over very low heat. When the top is clear of foam, simmer for 10 minutes. Then add the navet (turnips), cook for 10 minutes, and cook the potatoes for 10 minutes. The leeks and thyme sprig are cooked for another 10 minutes. Everything will have been cooked for 50 minutes, including the chicken. Check if it is cooked through; if not, add about another 10 minutes for the chicken. At that point, make sure that the vegetables are perfectly tender.

3. When the vegetables and chicken have cooked, remove from the heat and ladle out 300 ml/10½ fl oz/scant 1¼ cups of the cooking liquor straight into a sauté pan. Place over low heat, add 100 ml/3½ fl oz/1/3 cup + 2 tbsp of the cream and simmer until reduced by half. This should take about 10-12 minutes. While the sauce reduces, whip the remaining cream in a small bowl, add to the sauce, return to a simmer, and then turn the heat off. The sauce should just be thick enough to coat the back of a spoon. Add the black olives, lemon zest and a squeeze of lemon juice - check the seasoning before adding any more lemon juice. It should just be slightly lemony but not acidic. Add the picked thyme leaves and stir through.

4. Lift the chicken and potatoes out of the bouillon - you can use the bouillon and the remaining vegetables for soup. Discard the string, cut the chicken into four or six pieces and place it straight onto a serving plate. Crush the potatoes with a little olive oil, serve alongside, then spoon the sauce. Finally, sprinkle the flakes of almonds.

Roasted farmed rabbit legs with mustard and herbs cream

Serves: 6
Preperation time: 25 minutes
Cooking time: 1 hour 20 minutes

INGREDIENTS

1 large, farmed rabbit prepared by your butcher (1.6kg)

100 g/3 oz pancetta, diced and blanched

1 large onion, roughly chopped

2 garlic cloves, chopped

30 g/1 oz/butter

2 tbsp sunflower oil

4 tbsp Dijon mustard

250 ml/8 fl oz brown chicken stock

1 bunch of flat parsley

200 ml/7 fl oz white wine

Sea salt and freshly ground black pepper

1 tbsp plain flour

150 ml / 5 fl oz single cream

Since a very early age, when visiting my great aunt Suzanne, I have not only listened to stories about cooking in general but also helped in the small holding they had, feeding the animals, knowing that one day we were going to enjoy eating some of it, this was the way, but we looked after them like a king, if I may say, a farmed rabbit was one of those animals. In fact, we fed them only in the last few weeks with parsley. They loved it, making the flesh scented with that herb... oh my word, so delicious, hence why this recipe. MEMORIES!!

DIRECTIONS

1. Make sure the rabbit is cut for you.

2. With the help of a pastry brush, coat all the rabbit pieces with the mustard. Heat a large saucepan over a medium heat. When foaming, place all the coated rabbit pieces and roast gently.

3. When it starts to colour all round but not burnt, throw in the onion and pancetta and cook for a few minutes or until golden. Sprinkle in the flour and carry on mixing with a wooden spoon. It is now time to Deglaze with white wine and let it evaporate so you get rid of the acidity of the wine. Add the stock, the garlic, and half of the parsley, keeping the other half for chopping and sprinkling at the end.

4. Make sure you cover it, leaving a small gap, and only simmer for about 1 hour. Then, check that it's cooked; it should be soft and not quite falling off the bone at this stage. Remove the parsley stalks, check the seasoning, and you should have a lovely, silky juice, but not to reduce at that point. Add the cream and reduce slowly until it is like syrup or covers the back of a spoon.

5. Throw in the chopped parsley and season to taste. As you noticed, we did not add salt during the cooking process due to the pancetta, as even if it is blanched earlier, it could still be salty. That way, you avoid a salty dish due to the reduction.

6. Now serve hot with some tagliatelle, which is a great partner for that dish!

Marinated guinea fowl with ginger, lemon and garlic

Serves: 4
Preperation time: **Marinate overnight**
Cooking time: 1 hour plus

INGREDIENTS

1 guinea fowl (1.6 kg/3 lb 8 oz)

4 tbsp olive oil

2 small lemons, washed and sliced with skin on

1 head of garlic, each clove slightly crushed, skin on

1 bulb of fresh ginger, thinly sliced

2 sprigs of basil

1 small chilli, deseeded, cut in thin slices (use only half if too strong)

Sea salt and freshly ground black pepper

Since living in Singapore for a few years in the early 90s, I really like those three elements together. If dosed correctly, it brings a lot of fragrance, and the balance is lovely. It is often used in some of the food courts to a precise balance. I want to give guinea fowl a bit more credit, so I decided to use it in this recipe. It is now available in most supermarkets. It is a very great poultry, and it is a must-try for me.

I have done this a few times during lockdown. It works very well indeed; it's great comfort food!

DIRECTIONS

1. Take a large shallow tray and place half of the garnish in the bottom. Add prepared guinea fowl, put them in the tray and press down. Place the rest of the ingredients on the top, drizzle with olive oil, cover with cling film, press down once more, and place in the fridge overnight.

2. The following day, take it out 1 hour before grilling or roasting so it gets to room temperature. Preheat the oven to 180 C/350 F/Gas 4. Remove the cling film, and place the guinea fowl on the garnish on a cooking tray. Remove the basil and drizzle it with fresh olive oil, salt, and freshly ground black pepper. Make sure you turn it halfway through the cooking process until the skin is crispy but not burnt; the guinea fowl will take about 1 hour. Check it, and if you need a bit more, put it back for a few minutes or so. Baste it every 15 minutes to help the crispiness. Serve with some grilled vegetables and roasted new potatoes.

NOTE: Here I have cooked in a small casserole, guinea fowl breast as I used the legs for another recipe. The time is only 20-25 minutes cooking and the lemon is caramelised for sweeter flavour.

Caramelised apple and rosemary cake

Serves: 6-8
Preperation time: 20 minutes
Cooking time: 25-30 minutes

INGREDIENTS

PEARS:

100 g/3½ oz caster sugar

50 g/1¾ oz butter

2 large apples, peeled, halved, cored and roughly chopped

1 sprig of rosemary, needles picked and finely chopped

PLUMS (YELLOW, LARGE):

10 plums, halved, stoned, then cut into 6 segments each

100 g/3½ oz caster sugar

1 tbsp limoncello

CAKE:

100 g/3½ oz icing sugar

100 g/3½ oz butter

3 eggs

100 g/3¾ oz plain flour

1 tbsp raze baking powder

You cannot beat a nice, caramelised apple in a dessert, especially in the autumn when they are so tasty, the flavour is awesome. Roasted with flaked almonds in a tatin, for example, served with vanilla ice cream or simply on their own, but you will never enjoy them more than when they are caramelised slowly and folded into a cake mix. What a delight; the smell is incredible. It is everywhere in the kitchen.

Oh! I forgot, the herbs, which herbs? Well, it is in the recipe title, so I have to use that one, I guess. Of course, spices would also have been perfect with apples, but they did not feel right for the cake. I wanted some freshness to spread through the cake while it was cooking, so I didn't add the rosemary until after the apples were caramelised. They were just cooling, so the scent infuses the cake as it cooks. You'll see that it makes a big difference in taste.

DIRECTIONS

1. Start by cooking the apples. Place a frying pan over gentle heat, add the sugar and cook slowly until it turns to a light golden caramel. Add the butter, and only when it's foaming do you want to add the apples. Once more, it is essential that these are at room temperature; otherwise, the caramel will block - it will form lumps of hardened caramel, and then it's a matter of starting again! So, add them and cook until they are soft and caramelised. Remove from the heat, add the rosemary and toss to combine, then lay the apples onto a kitchen cloth to cool and dry out slightly - you want the cloth to absorb any juices.hence why the caramel should be still soft and not burn,as it would stick to the cloth.

2. While the apples cool, we can start the cake. You really want to do this in a machine, as the butter mixture needs to be really light in colour and texture. So, put the icing sugar and butter into a kitchen mixer and beat until almost white in colour and very light and fluffy using a paddle or electric whisk. Add the eggs, one by one, beating well between each addition. Sift the flour and baking powder into a bowl, then sift into the mixture, keeping back about 1/3. Add the apples into the reserved flour and toss to coat thoroughly, then fold them gently into the cake mix.

3. Spoon into the cake tin and place in the oven to bake for 25 minutes - open the oven and slide the shelf out. Check the cake with a skewer through the deepest part. If it comes out clean, then the cake is ready. If not, then slide back into the oven, bake for another 5 minutes, and check again.

4. Allow to cool for as long as you can wait, then cut a slice and serve with a cup of tea. And if were you, I'd sneak a slice quickly before everyone else smells it and wants some, too.

Paris-Brest cake with cocoa nibbed and coffee cream

Serves: 4
Preperation time: 45 minutes, plus infusing/
resting 40 minutes
Cooking time: 35 minutes

INGREDIENTS
CRÈME PATISSER WITH COCOA NIBBED:

270 ml/9 ½ fl oz/1 cup + 1 tbsp milk

25 g/1 oz cocoa nibbed

25 g/1 oz coffee beans

3 eggs

100 g/3 ½ oz caster sugar

25 g/1 oz corn flour

250 g/7 oz soft butter

CHOUX PASTRY:

½ ltr of water

180 g/6 ¼ oz butter

5 g/1/8 oz/scant 1 tsp salt

1 tbsp caster sugar

250 50 g/9 oz/2 cups plain flour

6 eggs, small to medium

A few drops of vanilla essence

2 tsp cocoa nibs

1tsp of lightly roasted and crushed coffee beans

What a beautiful classic dessert, made of choux pastry with a praline flavour.

This pastry was created in 1891 to commemorate the Paris Brest bicycle race, hence the circular shape representing the wheel. It became popular with the riders because of the energy it gave them due to the high calorific value, and now it is found in patisseries all over France. Here, I used cocoa nibs. I infused it into the cream and sprinkled it on the top of the pastry before baking. It will add a lovely bitterness when you crunch down on it, a very interesting addition that I hope you will love, this twist on the classic Paris Brest.

DIRECTIONS

1. Put the milk into a saucepan, place it over medium heat, and heat until it is just about to simmer. Add the cocoa nibs and coffee beans, remove from the heat, cover and set aside for 30 minutes to infuse.

2. While the milk infuses, make the choux pastry. Put the butter, salt, sugar and 500 ml/17 fl oz/2 cups water in a large saucepan and bring to a boil. Remove from the heat, add the flour and mix to combine using a whisk. Return to medium heat and stir gently with a wooden spoon until the mixture starts to dry, comes off the spoon easily and sweats slightly. Remove from the heat again and add the eggs one by one, whisking gently until the paste totally absorbs them. You should have a lovely yellow, silky mixture. Stir in the vanilla extract and set the pastry aside to rest for 35-40 minutes.

3. Preheat the oven to 180 C/350 F/Gas 4.

4. A tip for ensuring that you end up with a round Paris Brest is to take an 8 cm/3¼ in. plate and place it onto a sheet of greaseproof. Draw around the edge of it, then move it over by about 5 cm/2 in. and draw another. Repeat until you have 8 circles in total on the sheet. Remove the plate, turn the paper over, and place it onto a baking sheet ready to pipe.

5. Place the mixture into a piping bag, snip the end to 2 cm/¾ in. diameter, then carefully pipe onto the upturned paper 8 circles, taking care to use just one movement for each circle. If you interrupt the circle or movement, you will end up with a Paris Brest that you won't be able to fill! Sprinkle a little crumbled cocoa nibbed on the top of each circle.

6. Place the trays in the oven, but don't close the oven door completely. Put a wooden spoon on the top side of the oven, and then gently shut the door as far as it will go. This should leave a gap of about 5 cm/2 in. However, make sure that the oven is still working. The advantage of this is that with the door open, they will dry well as they cook and be very light. Sometimes, when you check to see how they are cooking, people will open the door too early and too far, and this will, in fact, stop the choux from rising. Sometimes, this is very obvious as they collapse immediately! They need to cook for about 30 minutes; by then, they will be medium golden brown and very light.

7. While the Paris Brest is cooking, make the patisserie - whisk the eggs, sugar and corn flour together for 5 minutes in a kitchen mixer or with an electric whisk in a bowl until light and fluffy. Strain the cocoa-infused milk onto the egg mix and whisk to combine, then pour back into the saucepan that the milk was in and return to the heat. Place over medium-low heat and stir continuously and quickly for about 10 minutes or until the mixture thickens. Remove from the heat and continue to stir until the mixture has cooled down and is lovely, smooth, thick, and slightly trembling.

8. Place the softened butter into the kitchen mixer or use an electric whisk once more and beat until very soft, then add the crème patisserie a little at a time until it is all incorporated. Beat them for about 10 minutes until it is very light and soft - a very light buttercream. You need to be careful at this point. You don't want the crème patisserie to be too warm and melt the butter; they both need to emulsify together at just above room temperature - if either is too warm, the mixture will split. If you see it start to split, don't add any more crème patisserie. Add a spoonful of room temperature water and beat until it emulsifies once more, then continue as before. It's a very delicate mixture and needs careful handling.

9. Now, it's time to assemble. Cut the Paris Brest in half horizontally, then place the top half immediately next to the bottom half. This helps you remember which half goes with which when you try to reassemble them. Spoon the filling into a piping bag, then using the same action as when you piped the Paris Brest, generously fill the pastry with the crème. Gently place the top back on to cover the cream, then dive in! Ideally, they should make it to the serving plate first before eating...

Clafoutis of infused linden tea with figs, peaches and plums

Serves: 6
Preperation time: 20 minutes, plus 1 hour
marinade time
Cooking time: 12 minutes if in ramequins,
25 minutes if in larger mould

INGREDIENTS

85 g/3oz soft, dry plums, roughly chopped

85 g/3 oz soft, dry figs, roughly chopped

85 g/3oz, dry peaches roughly chopped

90 g caster sugar

1 linden tea bag + 1 tbsp loose leaves

60 g/2 oz unsalted butter, half softened and
half melted

85 g/3 oz plain flour, sifted

1 pinch of salt

1 large egg

2 large egg yolks

200 ml/7 fl oz full-fat milk

80 ml/3 fl oz single cream

Clafoutis! Ahh, such a French favourite. This famous recipe was made with cherries originally, but because I also love those fruits together, I decided to give it a try and infused it with linden tea. Wow, it was great!!

DIRECTIONS

1. Put the soft, dry fruit into a bowl with the bag of linden tea. Make sure it is of great quality to have even more flavoured fruits. Cover it with warm water and let it cool for an hour or two so the fruits will soak well. Add the loose linden tea to the milk and let it infuse until you do the mix.

2. Preheat the oven to 180 C/350 F/Gas 4.

3. Strain the fruit. They should be soft by now and plumped. Keep aside. Discard the rest of the liquid and linden tea bag.

4. Grease a 24 x 16 x 6 cm (9 x 6 x 2 in.) in a baking dish or clafoutis dish (an oval earthenware dish) with the softened butter and sprinkle with 3 tbsp of sugar. Carefully shake the sugar around the dish to make sure it coats the inside.

5. Sift the flour and salt into a mixing bowl. Whisk the egg, egg yolks, and remaining sugar in a separate bowl.

6. Then, slowly add the mixture to the flour and mix until it is incorporated, silky, and smooth.

7. Slowly add the milk, which you have passed through a sieve to keep out the loose leaves, stirring until the batter has the consistency of a crepe mix, then add the melted butter and mix until combined.

NOTE: The fruits can be placed into either a clafoutis dish, a baking dish, or into ramekins. Spread them equally, then carefully pour the batter over it. Bake in a preheated oven for 25 minutes until set and golden brown. A tip of a knife inserted into it should come out clean and dry. Remove from oven and serve.

Beware when hot not to burn yourself with the caramel created on the side by the butter and sugar

Apple and blackberry puffs scented with rosemary

Serves: 6
Preparation time: 45 minutes
Cooking time: 12-15 minutes

INGREDIENTS

2 x 375 g/13 oz rolled all butter puff pastry, cut into 12 x fluted 7.5 cm/3 in. discs

4 large Bramley apples, peeled, halved, cored and roughly chopped

3 tbsp water

125 g/4½ oz fresh blackberries

1 sprig of rosemary, leaves picked and chopped

80 g/2¾ oz caster sugar

1 egg

1 pinch of salt

We made them at home and sometimes ate the rest on the way to school. You call them turnovers in Britain - the same idea, but it is done slightly differently. It is normally made with puff pastry, as you need this beautifully warm buttery crunch just before you reach the fruit, full of sweet acidity. For me, you need more fruit, that is for sure, but then it makes it tricky to close. So, make sure the mix is not too runny, as you cannot press it properly together. Blackberry and apple with rosemary are very delicate and fabulous together! Make enough of them as they will not last long, and don't forget, for sure, best eaten warm.

DIRECTIONS

1. Preheat the oven to 180 C/350 F/Gas 4.

2. Heat a large nonstick fryingpan over medium heat. Add the sugar, 2 tbsp of water and all the apples, cover them, and cook gently until they are cooked but not completely pureed. Remove the lid, then turn the heat up slightly so the liquid just starts to evaporate. Keep moving the apple around the pan with a spatula to help drive off the moisture and dry out the apple to have a dry puree. When it's dry, remove it from the pan and place it into a bowl to cool. (The puree must be dry and cold before you start to make your turnover; otherwise, the pastry will melt and collapse!) .

   Tip: Before you put the puree in, sprinkle some ground almonds. When cooking, they will absorb some of the remaining juice, so it stays drier.

3. Dust a work surface with a tiny bit of flour, then lay a disc onto the dusted surface and roll with a rolling pin, just once to the top and the bottom. You want the disc to just be slightly oval. Set aside, then repeat this with the other discs.

4. Mix the egg with the pinch of salt and the last tablespoon of water in a small bowl.

5. Lay all the discs out in front of you on the floured surface, with an oval shape going top to bottom. Place a spoonful of apple puree on the bottom third of the oval, leaving 1.5 cm/¾ in. from the sides. Place a few blackberries on top of the puree and a little sprinkle of rosemary, then brush the egg wash around the bottom edge of the oval - nothing so far has come above the halfway mark. Fold the top half of the pastry over to cover the filling, then gently press to seal the pastry edges. Brush the top of the pastry with the egg, taking care not to get any on the back of the folded pastry - this will run down and make the pastry stick to the tray! Using a spatula, carefully lift each one and place it onto a parchment or silicone-lined baking sheet, then use the back of a fork to make a crisscross pattern on top.

6.   Place it in the oven and bake for 12 minutes. Check at this point if the pastry is not golden brown, then return and cook for another 2-3 minutes.

7.   Remove from the oven and serve warm with a cup of coffee or Assam tea, ideally in front of the fire!

Thyme infused crepes with pink grapefruit and linden syrup

Serves: 4
Preperation time: 20 minutes, plus 45 minutes infusing
Cooking time: 25 minutes

INGREDIENTS

CREPES:

300 ml/10½ fl oz/scant 1 ¼ cup milk

2 sprigs of thyme

125 g/4½ oz plain flour

2 tbsp caster sugar

a pinch of salt

2 eggs

25 g/1 oz melted butter, plus extra for frying

LINDEN SYRUP:

100 g/3½ oz caster sugar

100 g/3½ ox butter

2 pink grapefruit, 1 zested and both juiced - you need 150ml/5floz

1 small handful of linden leaves picked

This is a twist on crepe Suzette; in fact, the origin of the dish and its name remain disputed. Was it a lady or girl who was involved, and her name was Suzette? This recipe was created in the late 19th century.

The most common way to make Suzette is to pour liquor, usually Grand Marnier, over it, sprinkle it with sugar and then ignite it. But here, we will just make a syrup with grapefruit infused with linden. You will see how different and delicious it is - don't forget to invite the family and have fun making them!!

DIRECTIONS

1. Firstly, infuse the milk - put the milk into a saucepan and bring to a boil. As soon as the milk boils, throw in the thyme, remove it from the heat, cover it with cling film, and leave it to infuse for 45 minutes until it cools. Discard the thyme.

2. While the milk infuses, make the syrup. Place a frying pan over a gentle heat, add the sugar and cook slowly until it turns to a light golden caramel. Add the butter, and only when it's foaming, add the grapefruit juice, mix well and bring to a simmer. Cook until it forms a syrup, then remove from the heat and throw in the linden. Leave to infuse in a warm place.

3. Put the flour, sugar, salt, eggs and 125 ml/4 fl oz/½ cup of thyme-infused milk into a bowl. Add the butter and whisk until smooth. Whisk in the remaining milk until it's smooth. Alternatively, if it's easier for you, just pop everything into a blender. Blend for a few minutes, then slowly add the rest of the milk and blend a little more. The important thing is to make sure that there are no lumps and the consistency is quite runny so that your crepes will be thin and light. When you do it gradually like this, there is no need to rest the batter.

4. Heat a 15-18 cm/6-7 in. non-stick pancake or frying pan over a medium heat. If you use a non-stick pan, you won't have to add butter to the pan as there is some already in the batter, though it can make the flipping easier if you do. If you're not using a non-stick pan, add a little butter to the pan first to keep the pancake from sticking.

5. Using a ladle, pour enough batter into the pan to cover the base thinly. Swirl the pan around to help spread the batter, if necessary, then cook for 1-1 ½ minutes. Now comes the fun part - try to flip it - or you can use a spatula. Cook for a further 1-2 minutes on the other side.

6. Remove the pancake from the pan and repeat with the remaining batter, adding more butter to the pan if necessary.

7. When all the pancakes have been cooked but are still warm, fold them in half one at a time and dip them very quickly into the linden-infused syrup. Swirl around slightly with tongs to ensure the pancake is coated with syrup, then fold over into quarters and serve immediately. Repeat with the remaining pancakes and syrup.

8. If you're really lucky, the last one will be for you!!

L'HIVER (WINTER)

Depending on where you live, cold wind, rain, and sometimes snow make up most of that season. Days are short, but we can still appreciate that beautiful white coat after a snowy day where sometimes the only footprint you can see is of a robin, a wild bird, or even deer, as, after all, it is the hunting season.

You can't beat a lovely log-burning fire to help you get cosy until some of your favourite winter dishes are served, from a gorgeous butternut squash soup to a roasted pheasant or even a simple hot chocolate. But why not a pear tatin or even an underrated roasted guinea fowl?

For now, trees are standing very still and bare, waiting for the signal of Spring, as shown by the first snowdrops or crocus.

Green lentils and pancetta soup with chives and mushroom cream

Serves: 4
Preperation time: 20-25 minutes
Cooking time: 35 minutes

INGREDIENTS

1 tbsp olive oil

100 g/3¾ oz pancetta, cut into small pieces

1 red onion, finely sliced

1 carrot, peeled and diced

1 bouquet garni made with 1 thyme sprig and 1 parsley sprig, tied together with kitchen string

200 g/7oz puy lentils, picked over and rinsed

1.2 litres/40 fl oz/4¾ cups vegetable stock or even chicken stock works well

150 ml/5 fl oz/scant/2/3 cup whipping cream

1 bunch of chives

40 g/1½ oz butter

100 g/3½ oz chestnut mushrooms, cleaned and sliced

Sea salt and freshly ground black pepper

Another winter warmer, this soup is very popular in my region. We do use lentils a lot, generally puy or green lentils. They are from Puy-En-Velay, in the Haute Loire, and have been awarded AOP (protected origin) since 2008. they first appeared in 1643 and are often called the caviar of the poor! I don't mind having this type of caviar as often as possible. This way, you can try them if you have not yet done so. Pancetta will bring some saltiness, as will a lovely earthy mushroom fricassee and fresh chives cream. Wow! So good.

DIRECTIONS

1. Heat a sauté pan over medium heat, add the olive oil and pancetta and sweat for 3-4 minutes until golden brown. When it's brown, add the red onion, carrot, and sweat for 2-3 minutes, then add the lentils and vegetable stock. Bring to a boil, turn the heat down and simmer for 10 minutes, then pour in 100 ml/3½ fl oz/1/3 cup + 2 tbsp of the whipping cream. Return to a simmer and cook for another 10 minutes or until the lentils are cooked through.

2. Ladle the soup into a blender and blitz until very fine. If the liquid quantity is correct and you have simmered the soup gently, it should be a lovely, shiny, creamy soup that is not heavy or sticky. If it is too thick, add a little water or more vegetable stock to let it down until it is velvety. Pour back into a saucepan, check the seasoning and keep warm.

3. Whip the remaining cream to soft peaks and fold in the chopped chive. Season with a touch of freshly ground black pepper.

4. Heat a frying pan until hot. Add the butter, and when it's foaming, add the mushrooms and sauté over high heat until golden brown, for about 3-4 minutes. Season with salt and black pepper, then add the rest of the chive.

5. Lay out four soup plates and divide the mushrooms between them in a little pile in the centre of the plate, then place a spoonful of cream on top of the mushrooms. Finally, ladle the lentil soup around the edge and into the bowls.

6. Serve with some crusty farmhouse bread.

Celeriac soup with mushroom fricassee and croutons

Serves: 4
Preperation time: 30 minutes
Cooking time: 50 minutes

INGREDIENTS

1 small celeriac, about 600 g/21 oz, peeled and cut into cubes, about 2 cm/¾ in.

2 tbsp olive oil

50 g/1¾ oz butter

1 small onion, chopped

1.2 litres/40 fl oz/4¾ cups vegetable stock

200 ml/7 fl oz/scant 1 cup whipping cream

200 ml/7 fl oz/scant 1 cup full-fat milk

75 g/2½ oz of mushroom

2 tbsp extra virgin olive oil

2 sprigs of chervil

I love celeriac. As a root vegetable, it is very versatile and makes a great soup that is easy and a fantastic winter warmer. I think it is coming back into fashion; it certainly is in my home, but you must be careful, as it can be hard to cut. First, the skin can be tricky to remove, so make sure you work from a nice, steady board, as your finger might be in the way, and you do not want that happening! When you make this, you will hopefully discover another lovely root vegetable which goes brilliantly with the caramelised mushroom fricassee and some croutons.

DIRECTIONS

1. Preheat the oven to 200 C/400 F/Gas 6.

2. Place the celeriac onto a roasting tray, drizzle with the olive oil and a touch of sea salt and black pepper, then roast in the oven for 12-15 minutes until just colouring around the edges but not cooked through yet. Remove from the tray and drain onto kitchen paper.

3. Meanwhile, heat a large sauté pan over medium heat, add half the butter and the onion, and sweat for 3-4 minutes until it softens but is not coloured. Add the roasted celeriac to the pan and toss together, then add the stock, cream and milk and bring to a simmer. Cook gently over low heat until very soft, in fact, overcooked - this will take about 30 minutes. The pan must not boil as this will curdle the soup.

4. While the soup cooks, make the mushroom fricassee. Heat a frying pan over medium heat. Add the last of the butter; when it's foaming, add the mushroom and cook until it starts caramelising but not burning for about 3-4 minutes. Check the seasoning, remove it, and place it aside in a warm place.

5. The soup should be ready now, so ladle it into a food blender and blitz until very smooth, then pass through a fine sieve back into a clean saucepan. Check the seasoning and warm back through - it should be very creamy and velvety, just like a veloute now. Add more stock to thin it slightly if it's a little thick.

6. Ladle into the soup plates, put some of the mushroom fricassees in the middle, and put a prig of chervil on each plate, finishing with a drizzle of extra virgin olive oil. Serve hot with some croutons.

NOTE: If you cannot find chervil, use a bit of coriander.

Roast monkfish fillet with saffron scented mussel ragout

Serves: 4
Preperation time: 35 minutes, plus cooking the rice
Cooking time: 30 minutes

INGREDIENTS

1 monkfish fillet, about 600 g/21 oz, skinless and boneless

1kg/2,6lb/42oz fresh mussels

2 tbsp of olive oil

55 g/2 oz butter

1 shallot, finely chopped A pinch of saffron threads

100 ml/31/2 fl oz/scant 1/2 cup double cream, half of it whipped Zest of 1 lime

1 small handful of chives, roughly chopped

Sea salt and freshly ground black pepper

Steamed rice to serve

I absolutely love the monkfish season. In the past, this fish was not featured on the menu or table due to its look. It is now becoming prime, and it is difficult to find some time. You must try roasted on the bone, as it is much more tasty, plus a very meaty fish, which is just delicious. Here, mussels cooked with saffron will lift the monkfish to an even better dish.

DIRECTIONS

1. Preheat the oven to 200 C/400 F/Gas 6, wrap the monkfish in a clean tea towel and set aside. This will absorb excess liquid and make it easier to roast.

2. Remove and discard the beard from the mussels and wash them under running cold water, scrubbing well to remove all traces of grit. Discard any that float or open ones that do not close when tapped. Set aside.

3. Put half the oil and butter in a medium-sized cast iron casserole over medium heat. When the butter begins to foam, add the monkfish and cook for 4-5 minutes, turning continuously, until it has a lovely golden colour all over. Transfer to the preheated oven and roast for 8 minutes until firm to the touch. Remove from the oven, transfer to a clean dish, cover with kitchen foil and set aside.

4. Put the remaining oil and butter in a cast iron or heavy-based pan over medium heat. When the butter is foaming, add the shallot and cook for 1 minute, stirring, then add the mussels and saffron. Cover and cook for 4-5 minutes or until the shellfish open. Discard any mussels that remain closed.

5. Pour the unwhipped cream into the pan with the shellfish and cook, uncovered, over medium to high heat, for 2 minutes. Remove from the heat, use a slotted spoon to remove the shellfish from the pan, put them in a large bowl, then cover and set aside. Return the pan with the cooking liquid to medium heat and cook for 4-5 minutes until reduced by half. Stir in the whipped cream and cook for a further 2-3 minutes. Remove from the heat, add the lime zest, chives, and any juices collected from the monkfish, and season with salt and pepper. You should now have about 100 ml/3 ½ fl oz/ scant ½ cup sauce.

6. Slice the monkfish into four pieces and either divide it into four plates with the ragout and a few spoonsful of the sauce spooned over it or place it in a casserole dish to serve at the table with steamed rice.

NOTE: You can now buy fresh coconut milk in the chilled section of the supermarket.

Poached hake in coconut milk infused with lemongrass

Serves: 4
Preperation time: 8 minutes
Cooking time: 20 minutes

INGREDIENTS

25 g/1 oz butter

1 tbsp olive oil

4 pieces skin on, boneless hake, about 150 g/5½ oz each

4 garlic cloves, skin on and lightly crushed

600 ml/21 fl oz/scant 2½ cups whipping cream

400 ml/14 fl oz/1½ cups + 2 tbsp coconut milk

1 lime zest and half the juice

Hake is often forgotten, yet in France, it is very popular. However, it's not eaten as much here as people prefer cod or haddock. Due to the overfishing of both species, hake is now more widely available and used. I am glad as it is also delicious.

Here, I have poached the fish in coconut milk to add a bit of an Asian accent, but not too much. The influence remains from my home, and I guess it will always be that way. Be careful when you poach it; it can be very fragile, and this is a flaky fish.so I recommend keeping the skin so it can hold the flesh better. To help that, I have roasted it first on the skin to give it a nice crispy, nutty flavour, which is very tasty, too, and lime zest will almost do the rest by bringing such a fresh taste to this.

DIRECTIONS

1. Heat the butter and olive oil in a nonstick frying pan until the butter has turned golden. Season the skin side of the fish with sea salt and black pepper, then place it in the pan with the crushed garlic, skin side down, and cook for 3-4 minutes until the skin is crispy.

2. While the fish is cooking, bring the cream and coconut milk to a simmer in a wide, shallow sauté pan - the liquid needs to be a touch below the height of the fish so the skin doesn't soften in the next stage of cooking. When the skin is crispy, flip the fish over, sprinkle with lime zest and place immediately into the simmering liquid, ensuring that the skin stays up and out of the liquid. Add the garlic cloves to the liquid and simmer for 8 minutes.

    Tip - to check that the fish is cooked, press lightly on the skin, and the flesh at the side starts flaking away.

3. At that point, remove the fish, place them on serving plates and cover them with cling film to keep them warm. Return the pan to the heat, and simmer until the liquid has reduced by at least half until it is thick enough to coat the back of a spoon, about 5-8 minutes. Add any juices collected from the resting fish, the rest of the lime zest and a few drops of lime juice. Check the seasoning, pass the sauce through a fine sieve and spoon over the fish.

4. This can be served with a nice mashed potato, made using the leftover sauce instead of milk.

Fillet of sea bream with caramelised orange and fennel

Serves: 4
Preperation time: 20 minutes
Cooking time: 25 minutes

INGREDIENTS

2 -medium fennel bulbs, as long as possible

25 g/1 oz butter

1 tbsp olive oil

1 orange, sliced

2 garlic cloves, crushed with skin on

1 tsp of fresh thyme leaves

2 medium-sized sea bream, about 800 g/1 lb 12 oz each, gills out, scaled and gutted

1 small red onion, finely chopped

1 tbsp chopped coriander leaves

½ tbsp chopped dill leaves

4 tbsp extra virgin olive oil

1 tbsp fig vinegar

In the past few years, I have done a lot of demonstrations around the country and have used sea bream and fennel at most of them in very different ways. The reason was to show how these two ingredients work so well together. What I did find, though, was that very few people cook with them. Firstly, you find the aniseed in fennel too strong, but mainly, you do not know what to do with fennel, or you do not normally use this fish either. Sea bream is very underrated, but it's a great sustainable fish and very affordable, as one is often enough for two people.

So, I recommend that you try this lovely yet refreshing recipe, as cooked fennel changes in taste compared to raw.

DIRECTIONS

1. Preheat the oven to 200 C/400 F/Gas 6.

2. Cut the top third of the fennel off and set it onto greaseproof paper over a foil on a medium baking tray. Peel off the first two layers, roughly chop and add to the tray. Place the orange slices and the garlic where you are going to sit the fish.

3. Heat a large nonstick frying pan over medium-high heat. Add the butter and olive oil, and when the butter is foaming, add the fish and pan fry on each side for 3-4 minutes. It should be a light golden brown and slightly crispy. A little tip: if you're not too sure how nonstick your pan is, place a sheet of double-sided greaseproof paper cut to fit the bottom of the pan, in the pan when it's hot, then add the butter, oil, and fish and cook in the same way - this will prevent it sticking, but will not make it hot enough to catch fire! Season with sea salt and black pepper, then place orange and garlic on top of the fennel. Spoon the cooking juices from the frying pan over the top of the fish, sprinkle with the thyme leaves, and place in the oven to roast for 12-14 minutes.

4. While the fish cooks, make the fennel salsa. Take the remaining fennel hearts and slice them very finely, using a mandolin if you have one, then place them in a large bowl with the remaining ingredients and toss to combine.

5. By now, the fish should be ready - insert a knife into the flesh, and it should slice through without any resistance. Remove from the oven and rest for 2 minutes while you place the fennel salsa onto the serving plates. Place the whole baking tray onto a trivet in the middle of the table to serve, allowing people to help themselves to the fish - you must lift the fish off the bone, and it will come away very easily. Then lift the whole bone from the tail end upwards, revealing the fillet on the other side and serve that too.

Serves: 4
Preperation time: 25 minutes
Cooking time: 2 hours 15 minutes

INGREDIENTS

600 g/1 lb 5 oz diced fatty pork neck

2 small carrots, peeled and chopped

2 shallots, chopped

1 sprig of thyme, leaves

2 garlic cloves, skin on, lightly crushed

100 ml/3 ½ fl oz/1/3 cup +2 tbsp white wine

500 ml/17 fl oz/2 cups brown chicken stock

1 tbsp chopped flat-leaf parsley

Sea salt and freshly ground black pepper

4 x 200 g/7 oz peeled King Edward or agria potatoes

20 g/3/4 oz butter

2 tbsp olive oil

I love all the forgotten parts of pork, beef, or lamb. They are so much tastier and quite a lot cheaper, too, which is a good enough reason on its own to use them! I'm using the neck as a good mix of meat and fat here, but it's much better braised than roasted. Be sure to ask your butcher to cut the pork into large cubes, but keeping the fat on will make the dish much more tasty and moister, which, for me, is essential. Remember, only use a fork to crush it partially when the meat has cooked. You are not doing a "rillette", which will give you a better flavour. Make sure you add the juices back in. It will be lovely and succulent, and you'll most likely be tempted to eat it there and then! But, you need to put it into a potato and a firm one like King Edward or agria, as it has to hold together. A touch of thyme will finish it perfectly, but be careful, as too much will spoil the dish.

DIRECTIONS

1. Preheat the oven to 140 C/275 F/Gas 1.

2. Heat a large casserole dish over high heat. Add the butter and 1 tbsp of olive oil, and when foaming, add the pork, carrots, shallot and garlic and roast together for 5 minutes until just browning. Add the white wine and deglaze until reduced by 2/3, then add the chicken stock and bring to a simmer. Cover with a lid or foil 9/10 ths of the way over. Cook over a low heat for 2 hours until the meat is very tender, not quite falling apart, stirring every 30 minutes. The sauce should be lovely and silky and coat the back of the spoon.

3. While the pork cooks, peel the potatoes and trim the base so it just sits flat on a board, then cut the top ¼ lengthways off and set immediately next to the potato. Scoop the inside flesh from the potatoes, leaving a 5 mm thick edge and taking care not to cut into it. You can discard the inside flesh or keep it for soup. Season the inside with salt and black pepper, and divide the tablespoon of olive oil between the four potatoes. Place the lid back on each of the potatoes and wrap each in cling film tightly, but you must ensure the potatoes stay all together. Cook in a steamer on a very low simmer for 35 to 40 minutes - the potatoes will be tender but beautifully white. Turn the heat off under the steamer, then leave for 10-15 minutes to finish cooking. They should now be perfectly cooked. But check with a small toothpick to make sure before you take the film out.

4. The meat should nearly be ready by now, so remove the potatoes from the steamer, cut the cling film, lift the potato lid off and turn the potato upside down onto a cloth to absorb any condensation, then place the potatoes base down onto a roasting tray. Remove the pork from the heat, take out 100 ml/3 ½ fl oz/1/3 cup +2 tbsp of the cooking juices and set aside into a bowl, then crush the meat with a large fork so that it forms a crumble sort of mix, not a paste, a little more texture left than that. Then, stir in the parsley and check the seasoning. Fill each potato with the mixture, taking care not to break the potatoes. Cover with the potato lid, then spoon the reserved juices over the top. Put in the oven for 15 minutes until hot and slightly bubbling. Serve with a lovely green salad. I really love those. Mum used to make them in a cold winter. So good!

Pork shoulder steak with chilli, ginger braised savoy cabbage.

Serves: 4
Preperation time: 25 minutes
Cooking time: 25 minutes

INGREDIENTS

2 tbsp sunflower oil

2 tbsp olive oil

4 pork collar steaks, about 160 g/6 oz each

90 g/3½ oz butter

2 garlic cloves, crushed with the skin

2 long red chillies, halved, seeded and finely chopped

1 pointed cabbage, quartered lengthways,
stem removed and shredded

50 g/2 oz fresh ginger, peeled and finely julienned

1 tbsp flat-leaf parsley, roughly chopped

Pork collar is very tasty due to the balance of meat and fat, so when it's pan-fried, it brings a lovely nutty flavour to the dish, enhancing the sauce, too. The secret of this dish lies in the braising of the cabbage. Here, I use pointed cabbage, which is very tender and will only need a few minutes of cooking, with the addition of chilli, ginger and fresh parsley. When it is all combined during that very short braising time, it will bring freshness to this delicious recipe... In fact, never mind the pork - just give me the cabbage!!

DIRECTIONS

1. Preheat the oven to 120 C/250 F/Gas 1.

2. Warm the oil in a non-stick frying pan over medium heat. Add the pork collar and cook for 4-5 minutes on each side until golden brown. Add 30 g/1¼ oz of the butter and the garlic when you turn them over. Remove from the pan, place on a plate and keep warm in the oven, setting the frying pan to one side.

3. Bring a saucepan of salted water to the boil, add the cabbage and return to the boil, then immediately drain and return to the empty saucepan. Add 1 ½ of the red chillies, all the ginger, and 30 g/1¼ oz of the butter, then season with salt and black pepper. Cover with the lid, return to a very low heat, and braise gently for 2-3 minutes, but no more. Remove from the heat and leave to infuse while you finish the sauce, just for 3-4 minutes.

4. Return the frying pan that the pork was cooked into the heat. When the juices are bubbling, add 100 ml/3¾ fl oz of water and cook until reduced by half. Whisk in the remaining butter a little at a time until the sauce has emulsified. Add the last ½ red chilli and half of the chopped parsley to the pan and stir through. Check the seasoning. Remove the pork from the oven and pour any resting juices straight into the sauce, stirring one last time.

5. It should all be ready to serve now. Add the last of the parsley to the cabbage, then the olive oil, check the seasoning and ensure the cabbage is still warm. Spoon the sauce over the pork. Then, serve the cabbage straight away.

Vegetables pot-au-feu with kohlrabi

Serves: **6**
Preperation time: **25 minutes**
Cooking time: **1 hour 30 minutes**

INGREDIENTS

3 tbsp rapeseed oil
8 carrots, washed, peeled and chopped
2 small leeks washed, chopped
2 onions, peeled, keep whole
6 cloves
1 bay leaf
1 kohlrabi, washed, cut into small segments
1 small swede, washed, peeled, diced
2 courgettes, washed, cut in half and chopped
Sea salt and freshly ground black pepper
1 sprig of thyme
1 sprig of parsley
2 sprigs of chervil, chervil

Kohlrabi, a lovely vegetable, which is often not known, or more often, we do not know what to do with it, is a kind of cross between cabbage and turnip, purple or whitish pale green in colour, but delicious when cooked and grated into a salad or roasted with venison. It's so much more versatile than we think. I like it in autumn and winter in a nice casserole.

DIRECTIONS

1. To make your bouillon, keep all the vegetable trimmings and onion skins. Add the rapeseed oil, and when it starts to get hot, add all vegetable trimmings. Roast well until golden brown, but do not go over that, as it will make the stock bitter. Add 3 litres of water, the bay leaf, thyme and parsley, and cook to simmer for 6-8 minutes. The stock should have a nice amber colour and good flavour at that stage. Then, place another heavy pan on the stove and pass the liquid through a sieve to collect only the stock. Keep the vegetable trimming for your compost, keeping only a bay leaf.

2. Now add all the lovely fresh vegetables and cook for about 6-8 minutes or until vegetables are soft but still have a slight bite to it is best to follow the order of texture from hard to soft, for example, carrots, then swede, then kohlrabi, etc., and check your seasoning.

3. Serve hot in deep bowl plates with the vegetables and throw in the chopped chervil. Add some lovely sourdough croutons to serve.

Gluten free chocolat and black pepper fondant

Serves: 4
Preperation time: 20 minutes, plus 20 minutes resting
Cooking time: 5-8 minutes

INGREDIENTS

100 g/3½ oz 70% dark chocolate
100 g/3½ oz butter
3 eggs
40 g/1½ oz caster sugar
40 g/1½ oz corn flour
1 tsp of Szechuan pepper

Chocolate fondant is a recipe that is often used in restaurants. It is done in many ways, with many different flavours or spices added or even infused, but the main idea or purpose is always the same. When it's cooked and turned out, the warm chocolate must find its way out, running slowly like lava coming down a volcano face. That is a must, but there is no compromising when it comes to the chocolate you are using. It must be good, not too sweet, not too bitter, and it must be dark. This recipe is scented with Szechuan pepper, but if you do not like that, you can use star anise, cinnamon, or cardamom. But use it carefully, as you only want to guess it is in it.

DIRECTIONS

1. Preheat the oven to 220 C/425 F/Gas 7.

2. Butter and cocoa, four small ramekins or pudding moulds.

3. Put the chocolate and butter into a bowl in the microwave and heat until melted. Cook according to manufacturer's guidelines; alternatively, place it over a saucepan of simmering water and leave until melted. Stir to combine, then set aside and keep warm away from the heat.

4. Whisk the eggs and sugar together for at least 15 minutes, either in a food mixer or in a bowl with an electric whisk, until they are almost white in colour, very shiny and nearly at a soft peak stage. (NB - the reason for whisking the eggs to this stage is that it will give a light crusty outside to the fondant, but the inside will melt soft.) Pour the melted chocolate and butter into the mix and whisk to combine. Sift the corn flour over the top and fold it, then finally fold the Szechuan in, taking care not to overmix it at this point - the mixture should still be warm. Divide the mixture between the ramekins, filling only ¾ full. Place them on a tray in a cool place to rest for 30 minutes.

5. Place in the oven and bake for 5-6 minutes - you want to see that the fondant has risen above the mould and has formed a light crust on top and around the edge. Remove and turn out straight onto a serving plate, then serve it immediately. It goes well with cinnamon crème anglaise!, or coffee.

NOTE: With the crème Anglaise, I have added a pinch (but not too much) of freshly diced chili, it goes very well.

Camomile infused rice pudding with prune marmalade

Serves: 4
Preperation time: 5 minutes
Cooking time: 20-25 minutes

INGREDIENTS

RICE PUDDING:
110 g/3¾ oz Carnaroli risotto rice

500 ml/17 fl oz/2 cups whole milk

200 ml/7 fl oz scant 1 cup whipping cream

2 chamomile flower teabags

60 g/2½ oz caster sugar

PRUNES MARMALADE:
250 g/9 oz blackberries

60 g/2½ oz caster sugar

My mum used to make it so often that I did not want to eat it anymore for a long time. In fact, I am only just starting to eat it again, as I love this recipe. For some reason, chamomile tea brings it to life. In the restaurant, we use carnaroli rice, the same as we use for risotto. I think it is the perfect grain for it, strong enough, nutty enough, too. So, cook it gently with all the other ingredients, and it will taste delicious, but you might have noticed that I said gently. It must be that way, as the grain will explode, and the mixture will burn if you have the heat too high, so be careful, and it will be a success. Serve with prunes marmalade over it. Superb!

DIRECTIONS

1. Make the rice pudding first. Place the rice, milk, cream, and teabags into a medium saucepan, stir once to make sure that all the rice is dispersed through the liquid, and then bring to a boil over medium heat. Turn the heat down to a simmer and cook for 18 minutes - you shouldn't need to stir, but just check a couple of times.

2. While the rice is cooking, make the prune marmalade. Place the prunes and sugar into a nonstick frying or sauté pan, place onto low heat and cook gently, stirring occasionally, until no juice is left and the blackberries are fully cooked - this should take about 10-15 minutes to be done properly. You want the prunes to release their juices simultaneously as they cook, so they need to be kept at a low temperature, so do not increase the heat. Eventually, they will dehydrate and turn into marmalade.

3. Turn the heat off. There should be a little liquid left in the saucepan. Take the teabags out and squeeze them dry over the saucepan so the liquid goes into the rice, but do not pierce the teabags!! Only once that's done do you want to add the sugar and fold it delicately into the rice. Keep turning the rice, but very gently, for 4-5 minutes to cool the rice down.

4. Spoon the rice immediately onto a serving bowl and top with some of the fresh prune marmalade.

NOTE: In the picture, the jar of prune marmalade I am holding was made by my sister Dolores with a written label. She makes a mean marmalade jam (confiture).

So GOOD!!!

You can serve some lovely, warm honey madeleine to accompany this rice pudding.

Bitter chocolate mousse, citrus fruits, zest and herbs

Serves: 4
Preperation time: 30 minutes
Chilling time: 1 hour
Cooking time: 25 minutes

INGREDIENTS

1 orange,washed, peeled, skin cut into zest

1 pink grapefruit Washed, peeled , skin cut into zest

1 lime ,wahed,peeled , skin cut into zest

100 g/3.5 oz/1 cup caster sugar

100 g/3.5 plain chocolate chips (66-70% cocoa)

3 egg yolks

150 g/5 fl oz /scant 2/3 cup double cream

1 tbsp icing sugar

1 small pinch of fresh coriander leaves

Most of us love a little bit of gorgeous chocolate, the combination of bitter chocolate and citrus fruits, which are one of my friends and family's favourites. I can tell you that it does not last long, which is why I make double batches. I have, too. Here, we will use 70% pure cocoa, but you can use less if it is too bitter or even dark milk at 55%. Watch out for disappearing chocolate in your home when you are not looking!

DIRECTIONS

1. Pare the zest of the fruits into strips with a zester, cutting any pith away, then with a small knife, cut them into medium-sized julienne. Put the zest in a small saucepan, cover it with cold water, and bring it to a boil over medium heat. As soon as it starts to boil, remove it from heat, refresh it under a cold water drain, and start the process once more.

2. Return zest to the pan using the same pan, and add 2 tablespoons of the caster sugar and 4 tablespoons of water, stirring to dissolve.

3. Bring to a boil and cook for 4-5 minutes or until zest becomes transparent, then leave the zest strips to cool in the syrup. When cold, drain and keep syrup.

4. To make the chocolate mousse, put 75 g/2 oz of the chocolate in a heatproof bowl and rest it over a saucepan of gently simmering water, making sure the bottom of the bowl does not touch the water.

5. Heat for 4-5 minutes, stirring occasionally, until the chocolate has melted. Remove from the heat, but keep warm. Mix the remaining sugar, egg yolks, and 4 tablespoons of warm water in a separate heatproof bowl. Rest the bowl over a saucepan of gently simmering water, making sure it does not touch the water. Beat the mixture for 8-10 minutes until it turns pale, thickens and forms a ribbon-like shape when you lift the whisk, and the mixture falls back into the bowl. Slowly stir in the melted chocolate until well combined.

6. In another bowl, whip the cream and icing sugar until soft to medium peaks form, then gently fold into the chocolate and egg mixture until you obtain a lovely smooth mix, taking care not to over-mix it. Divide the mousse into four glasses, glass dish or large ramekins, cover with a film, and chill for an hour. If chilled longer, remove from fridge 30 minutes before serving.

7. Before serving, melt the remaining chocolate in a heatproof bowl over simmering water, swirl over each mousse, top with the citrus zest, and add some micro coriander or broken coriander leaves.

NOTE: Mix all the citrus fruit segments with the syrup you kept aside to serve with the mousse if you like. Using fresh tarragon is another herb option that goes well with chocolate.

Warm chocolate cookies biscuits, vanilla ice-cream

Serves: 4-6
Preperation time: 25 minutes
Cooking time: 6-8 minutes

INGREDIENTS

150 g/5½ oz 60% dark chocolate, melted
100 g/3½ oz butter
2 eggs, separated
50 g/1¾ oz caster sugar
75 g/2½ oz plain flour
1 pinch of salt
1 handful of mini milk chocolate chips

YOU'LL NEED:

1 rectangular mini-hole silicone tray

Preperation time: 10 minutes, plus
20 minutes infusing
Cooking time: 10 minutes, plus freezing

INGREDIENTS

115 ml/3¾ fl oz/½ cup whole milk
1 fresh vanilla pod, split and seeds scraped
3 egg yolks
200 ml/7 fl oz/¾ cup + 2 tbsp double cream, whipped to soft peaks

Almost everyone loves cookie-type biscuits and ice cream, especially vanilla, except this one is beige. The reason is the use of a lot of the seed! So powerful goodness. Also, when it comes to chocolate, use the best you can. There is a big difference in flavour and taste, so 60/70% of cocoa is what to aim for, and dark milk is milk with a high cocoa content.

DIRECTIONS

WARM CHOCOLATE COOKIES BISCUITS

1. Preheat the oven to 220 C/425 F/Gas 7.

2. Melt the chocolate and butter in a saucepan over a gentle heat.

3. Whisk the egg yolks and sugar together until doubled in volume, thickened and a pale yellow colour - about 5 minutes. When the chocolate is melted, fold the flour straight into it until properly combined - you must be very careful when doing this, and use a wooden spoon or spatula and work quite quickly. Then, pour the chocolate mixture slowly onto the eggs and fold together.

4. Whisk the egg white with the salt until soft peaks form, then fold into the chocolate mixture. When it is ready, spoon into the mould, just half filling each hole, sprinkle with the milk chocolate chips, then bake in the oven for 6-8 minutes.

5. Remove from the oven and turn straight out onto a wire rack to cool.

6. Now, if you fancy making ice cream rather than buying it, here is the recipe

BROWN VANILLA ICE CREAM

1. Place the milk, vanilla pod and seeds into a saucepan and bring to a simmer. Turn the heat off immediately so it simmers, cover with cling film and leave to infuse for 20 minutes.

2. Remove the vanilla pod, wash it, and pat it dry on a kitchen towel. Reserve it to make your own vanilla sugar.

3. Whisk the egg yolks and warm milk together over a pan of simmering water until thickened and quite firm. When the sabayon is ready, remove from the heat and whisk continually until the mixture is cool. Fold the whipped cream into the cooled mixture - it needs to be cool enough that the cream won't melt when it is added. This gives you a lovely silky texture. Pour into a small flat mould, cover with cling film and place into the freezer until firm.

ACKNOWLEDGEMENTS

I want to thank my friends and family, but particularly my suppliers, Johnny and his team from Flying Fish. Joe and Ben from Smith & Brock. Kate Laffite, my photographer, and the entire team at Found. A special thanks also goes to my sister DOLORES for making this gorgeous plum jam I served with the camomile rice pudding, along with a handwritten label. So lovely!! It would not have been possible without your support. Much appreciated.

SMITH & BROKE

Founded in 2016 by brothers Joe and Nick, Smith & Broke is a fresh fruit and vegetable, dairy, dried, and fine foods wholesaler based in London. Having worked in the industry from a young age, Joe and Nick grew frustrated with the corporate way of looking after customers and procuring produce, leading them to start Smith & Brock with a simple purpose and philosophy: "To have the best people supplying the best product with the best service at the right price to customers, who value these attributes in a supplier."

They have searched far and wide to ensure they work with the best; from the Marché International de Rungis, growers from the coast of Italy and the mountains of Spain to the Kent countryside, they work with growers who produce the best quality products and have a passion for what they do.

FLYING FISH

Founded in 2006, Flying Fish serves some of the greatest chefs in the UK. We stick strongly to the ethos of delivering the best seafood the country has to offer to the best restaurants within 48 hours of being caught: 'Ship to Plate in 48'.

Every weekday morning our expert buyers are up before sunrise to pick the best catch from the Day Boats at Looe, Brixham, Newlyn and markets.

From Native Cornish Lobsters and Dover Soles to Offshore Deep-Sea Mussels, sourcing from local fisherman is key to providing not only the freshest fish, but also vital in supporting the community; mixing with the people who catch them, gives us a real insight into how important their history has been in creating the current industry we love.

KATE LAFITTE

KATE LAFITTE

Kate is a food photographer who lives in Cheshire with her husband and daughter. Originally from South London, Kate worked in event management for 15 years before deciding to combine her love of food and creativity and start her own business in food photography.

Since then, Kate's work has taken her to restaurants and businesses across London, Manchester, Birmingham, Wales and Switzerland and this will be the second cookbook she has photographed.

You can see more of Kate's work on her Instagram page @kate.lafitte or her website katelafittephotography.com

FOUND

Found are changing the publishing landscape by helping content creators turn their passions into income. Unlike traditional publishers, they support hundreds of creators by taking their social media content and transforming it into beautifully crafted books in as little as eight weeks.

Their sustainable print-on-demand model provides creators with a straightforward, risk-free way to earn from their digital content, no upfront costs, stocking, or excess inventory required.

www.found.us